THE HAPPY BARN CAT
RESCUING AND RAISING HEALTHY WORKING CATS

MELODI GRUNDY

WITH CONTRIBUTIONS FROM STEPHAN GRUNDY {MASTER HERBALIST}

ISBN: 978-1-959350-16-3
Set in: Georgia 14/18 bold/italic, Carnivalee Freakshow 38pt/29PT

©The Three Little Sisters LLC
USA/Canada

Contents

DEDICATION

The Happy Barn Cat is dedicated to two of our founding colony members here at Kilmurry House: Prince Mordred and Maude Catkin. Prince Mordred was a fine large (if tailless due to a dog encounter) brown-ticked spotted tabby gib-tom, born in a 14th-century Irish castle and hand-raised with an eyedropper when his mommy had no milk. He saved the lives of his friends on several occasions, including defending them from much bigger toms with murderous intent, and warning us when one of them took very suddenly sick near unto death.

He was also known for supervising many projects in our workshop, usually by draping himself helpfully about the shoulders of the person working. Prince Mordred ruled our barnyard for many years. Maude Catkin was a tidy little black-and-white girl who made a tom out of a young purebred male who couldn't figure out which end of his previous virginal purebred female was relevant to breeding. She bore three beautiful kittens, taught many others to hunt, and was one of the mightiest rat-slayers ever to stalk on four paws. Both of them passed quietly to Catnipping Green after very long lives. They have been gone for some time, but they are still deeply missed.

Authors Residence in Kilmurry House, Ireland

INTRODUCTION

De Laguna, Sr., who visited the Tlingit people on Wrangell Island in 1892 describes how "cats... flourished as if in an Egyptian temple. But the cats, dishonest like all of their tribe, were kept ignominiously tied by short ropes. They stole the fish, we were told, which fish, by the way, hung like portiéres all about the cabins" (p. 35). The Tlingit also called women who kept cats, particularly elderly ones, "Cat's mother" (Emmons, p. 139). One may wonder if these ladies served a purpose similar to that of the ferret- or ratting terrier-keeper in the Irish or English village: the person who would bring their furry rodent slayers around for request or hire to deal with acute infestations. De Laguna, Sr., who visited the Tlingit people on Wrangell Island in 1892 describes how "cats... flourished as if in an Egyptian "cats... flourished as if in an Egyptian temple. But the cats, dishonest like all of their tribe, were kept ignominiously tied by short ropes. They stole the fish, we were told, which fish, by the way, hung like portiéres all about the cabins" (p. 35). The Tlingit also called women who kept cats, particularly elderly ones, "Cat's mother" (Emmons, p. 139). One may wonder if these ladies served a purpose similar to that of the ferret- or ratting terrier-keeper in the Irish or English village: the person who would bring their furry rodent slayers around for request or hire to deal with acute infestations.

Dogs are humankind's oldest animal ally. They go back to the days of hunting and gathering, when a few low-ranking wolves discovered that living with humans and helping them chase game or warning them of danger in return for a share of the food was a much better deal than life for a wolf at the bottom of the pack. Until humans began to plant and store grain, there was no real need for cats – and then they became necessary indeed, as hunters of the vermin that could destroy a year's labor for food in a short time. The contract between farmers and cats goes back at least nine thousand years and may be even older. As soon as people begin to settle down and grow crops, they also needed to store them for later use. Staying in one place with food stored nearby inevitably attracted vermin such as mice and rats.

Small African and Asian cats saw this food as their natural prey and were delighted with the granaries. There was enough prey for colonies of cats to settle in one location. Most cats, big or small, enjoy the company of their own kind, provided their territories have enough food to support them all. The prototype barnyards of the Neolithic provided both abundant food and feline companionship. From the viewpoint of the cats, they were wonderful places to settle. Over time, cats became less afraid of the big creatures who shared their new territories. And the people realized that where cats were, the mice and rats were not. So they accepted the new arrivals. In Egypt, land of some of the world's first food storage centers, cats' roles were so important that they became little divinities. A very recent discovery of a cat buried with a high-status personage in Cyprus shows they were valued there as early as 9500 years ago.

> *"Cats lived violent lives and often died bloody deaths, always just below the usual range of human sight... Violent lives, violent deaths. A dog got them and ripped them open instead of just chasing them...or another tom got them, or a poisoned bait, or a passing car. Cats were the gangsters of the animal world, living outside the law and often dying there. There were a great many of them who never lived to grow old by the fire."*
> *– Stephen King, Pet Sematary, p. 50.*

Cats are not native to Cyprus, so they must have been carried there in boats, probably as part of a mainland farmer's usual package of livestock and seed plants. Other excavations in Malta show that, seven thousand years ago, new settlers also took their cats with them. Both early villages, cats had to be imported to the islands they were found buried in. These cats may have been some of the first felines in a long tradition of the Ship's Cat, whose descendants would follow generations of sailors across all the oceans of the world, providing vital pest control services as well as serving as mascots and favored pets.

Later barn cats would evolve into temple cats, shop cats, and even Post Office Cats. Before the modern era, most cats were seen as working animals first, and pets second. Even the Egyptians, whose wall paintings show court ladies with delicate cats on leashes eating fish beneath their feet, also show paintings of working cats retrieving birds for a hunter in his boat. This early artwork shows that cats (like dogs) quickly became friends with people as well as their working partners. The farmer today who laughs at the antics of barn kittens running up and down the hay loft is sharing something with his ancestors thousands of years ago.

As does his little girl when she brings one of the kittens into the house with big eyes saying, "Mommy, can I keep it?" (It's probably no accident that grown domestic cats are about the same size as a human baby, with big eyes, a round head, and a plaintive baby-like cry)...A great many cats also served their countries, or at least their adopted humans, in war. The horrors of the rat-infested trenches of WWI were mitigated by the cats who followed the rodents there (and, more sadly, also were deployed as "mine canaries" at times, being more susceptible to gas than humans).

The naval vessels of both World Wars had their cats, on whom the sailors depended for rodent control, morale, and, indeed, "luck" "(Banks). Some well-known Royal Navy cats included the famous Blackie, who served on HMS Prince of Wales (a battleship playing a significant role in several WWII actions), became a personal friend of Churchill's when his ship carried the politician to a Newfoundland meeting with Roosevelt, and was renamed after a picture of him with the politician became famous.

The black-and-white Convoy served on the escort ship HMS Hermione and, with the rest of Hermione's crew, died a hero when the ship was sunk in 1942. A luckier ship's cat was Unsinkable Sam, who survived having three ships torpedoed out from under him in fairly close succession - at which point the Royal Navy decided that his services might be better employed as the chief rodent control engineer for the office of Gibraltar's governor-general. Unsinkable Sam eventually retired to the Home for Sailors in the UK, where one might hope that he even met some of his old surviving shipmates again. (Brever)" In rural Ireland, however, it was not traditional for many generations to keep cats as pets.

They were seen as working farm animals, useful as rodent control but not treasured like the family farm dog. A few observations showed that here (as well as traditionally in much of the US and Britain) barn cats were not being fed any cat food. People believed that cats who were provided with food would not hunt. It was also (until very recently) so expensive to spay or neuter a cat that a cash-conscious farmer would never even consider it.

Extra kittens were simply drowned, not because people were cruel, but because the only other option was being overrun with cats. Since extra feral cats will often just wander away, the colony could appear to be staying the same size, when in reality there were too many cats for all of them to live well. Unfed and often over-populated, the cats became unhealthy and unkempt. This made them more likely to be dirty and carry diseases.

On many farms, it is the children who are the natural tamers of young kittens. But dirty and diseased animals made cautious mothers forbid their children to play with them. The ignored kittens would then grow up to be feral and afraid of people. The result is that barn cats were thought of as feral, dirty, and unsafe animals. The situation became a self- fulfilling prophecy created by ignorance and maintained long-standing practice of the barn cat being the only working animal on the farm that was pretty much ignored by the farmer.

The medical information in this book is largely courtesy of my husband Stephan Grundy, who is a health-care professional and medical researcher as well as an author. Any queries on the medical topics covered in this book should be directed to him – or run by your local vet (except for the potential feline uses of cannabis, which your vet cannot legally prescribe, recommend, or advise on regarding anything other than treatment for an excessive dose until there has been more official animal testing).

This is in large part a book about feral cats of various sorts and how to tame them, keep them healthy, and make them into friends or, where needed, working partners in the continuous war between humans and vermin. My husband and I have both lived and worked with cats of various sorts all our lives, from wild barn cat colonies to house-raised purebreds: this book has grown from our experience and those of our cats.

When my husband (a city boy with a long history of keeping pedigreed house cats) and I moved to the Irish countryside over twenty years ago, our first experience with the way locals handled barn cats summed up the whole country cat problem. We had gone to pick up some chickens from a nearby farmer. While Husband was bagging the birds, I saw a cat with a beautiful long-haired marmalade kitten and crouched down to talk to them. When I asked if there were any other kittens, the farmer said, "Oh, the dog got the others. Do you want it? I'll just have to drown it if you don't."

We went home with a cat. Eventually the word got out that we were suckers for excess kittens, and we ended up with fourteen or fifteen Irish moggies1, plus the breeding stock of Norwegian Forest Cats that Husband had imported at great effort and expense from Sweden. We got cats in various stages of feral behavior, from "extremely friendly" to "hide under the bed and run when people come", and managed to tame every one of them.

To the point that, when I go for walks down our lane way, I often have a fifty-yard train of cats trotting after me, one by one...and the Irish think I'm a witch, or mad, but without our horde of cats, we'd either have to put down enough rat poison to kill any army of your choice, or wake up to little scaly feet running over our faces in the night. As a result of the different approaches of ourselves and our neighbors, local folk were (and are) often stunned when they meet our barn cats. Ours are clean, healthy, friendly, and fat, and they catch vermin! The observer often follows their initial surprise by saying; *"Next time you have any kittens, I want one..."*

They are confused when we explain that we almost never have kittens, except for the occasional stray or orphans on the doorstep. But we also tell people, that they, too, can have happy, healthy, friendly working cats. They can start out simply, by feeding them and paying their cats some human attention. Then look at providing them with shelter from the elements and some rudimentary veterinary care. People are amazed by the results if they start doing this.

1-"'Moggy', sometimes shortened to "mog", is originally a British term, used frequently throughout the Commonwealth. It can be used as a generic for any cat (you could refer to someone's purebred Persian as "your moggy", or one could speak of "ordinary moggies" and "purebred moggies", meaning actual pedigreed cats), but when used specifically, is the feline equivalent of "mutt" or "Heinz 57" (a common American reference, suggesting 57 different breeds in the genetics). As in "What breed is your cat?" "She's a moggy/100% moggy".

For ourselves, we are careful not to re-home extra cats with anyone we don't think will follow through on these basic procedures. It takes time to overcome centuries of belief and practice, but it can be done. Even if it's slowly, one barnyard at a time, while I learned of these problems after moving to Ireland, the plight of ignored barn cats is as true in rural America as it is on Irish farmsteads.

Worldwide, the status of barn cats (and other farm animals) is slowly improving, as farmers and smallholders pay more attention to the health and welfare of the animals entrusted to their care. This book is intended as a guide to help farmers, smallholders, and other folk living in the countryside to continue this happy trend.

Whenever and wherever possible, donate to rescues that work on preserving, protecting and advocating animal welfare. The author and publisher have provided a list of suggested organizations some of which helped collect data and image for this book. As cat lovers, both the author and publisher wish to express that in all things, preserving and creating a happy life for your companions is a critical function of animal ownership.

DISCLAIMER

This book is not meant to be an alternative to seeking advice from your own veterinarian or animal health care provider. The author and publisher have provided, where possible, the background resources and research papers which should be researched independently so that the reader can form their own view.

The material in this book is a collection of knowledge from personal experience of the author who has spent a great deal of time and energy in preserving the health and welfare of cats. Some summations in this book may be disturbing to some readers if they are sensitive to the practical decisions of farm life. Farms are not run like urban households and therefore readers should understand that facts stated in this book reflect the real, sometimes harsh, choices made on a farm.

The 5 Basics

EAT, PURR, LOVE

FOOD AND WATER

SHELTER

AFFECTION

BIRTH CONTROL

BASIC MEDICAL CARE

For at least 9,000 years, farmers have relied upon the humble (or likely not so humble) barn cat as a primary defense against mice, rats and other vermin. They are a natural means of pest control, vital to agricultural storage.

That they also can delight us and be our friends is something that has developed over thousands of years. With a few modern adjustments, it's possible for a farmer or small-holder to have a happy, useful, and relatively healthy colony of barn cats who hunt for pleasure and have longer and better lives than their forebears. The three basic secrets are: Regular Meals, Birth Control, and Basic Medical Care (spaying, neutering, and vaccinations). There are other things such as human-cat interaction (petting the cats) and re-homing non-hunters, but these are the primary aspects.

How The Working Cat Works

In spite of all large-scale agriculture and herding do to feed us now, dogs still hunt and guard; and in spite of all the poisons and traps we have developed, cats are still important allies in the ongoing war between humans and rodents. They go where traps cannot reach; they patrol wide territories, dealing not only with the rodents that have set up to colonize barn and house, but those coming in from the wild. Even the smell of a cat is a significant deterrent to rats and mice.

The two that had shared our bedroom in our first house in Ireland were house-raised and had never caught a rodent in their lives, but their mere presence had been enough to keep the hordes away for a year. We found this out when we moved from our first countryside house to the second: the cats moved first, and less than a week after they were gone, Husband woke up to find himself staring into a pair of black beady eyes and a pointy nose attached to the biggest rat that he (city boy, remember) had ever seen in his life. He responded in a manly and heroic fashion, i.e.: screaming, "AAAGH! Get that thing out of here!"

The rat, presumably equally startled, fled for its life. After that, until we returned to the protection of our cats, we would lie awake listening to the rustling in the walls, wondering when the next brave rodent would make a kamikaze attack on our bed. When you are looking for working cats, it is important to remember that, for cats, hunting is partially instinctive, partially learned. All cats, whether they have ever seen a mouse in their lives or not, will pounce on a piece of string skittering across the floor, and will bring down rolls of toilet paper and kick them to death. But this doesn't mean that they will know what to do when they find a real rodent, as proven by the experience of two house-raised purebred queens from hardy barn-cat derived breeds (Trolle the Norwegian Forest Cat and Valkyrja the Maine Coon) who were completely baffled by a bat.

The most certain way to get a good mouser is to find a young cat whose mother is a good mouser. This will probably hold for all cats taken from the wild after eight to ten weeks or so, as a feral cat that cannot hunt will not have survived. It is not the only way. Our barnyard ruler, Prince Mordred, never caught a mouse until he was a year old, since until our move we lived close to the road and kept all the cats indoors; his mother had been beyond useless. But shortly after he started going out, he became an excellent hunter, probably through observing the other cats we had adopted from barnyards.

The size of a cat is not a guarantee of its skill as a hunter, either. Two of our best-ever ratters, Maud and Ragnar, both started bringing in huge rats at three to four months old – huge rats, nearly the same size as the young cats. Maud, a neat and sweet-tempered little black-and-white short-haired moggie, was very nearly our smallest female; Ragnar was the smallest male we have had; but both were tremendously efficient and dedicated rat-slayers.

Both started life as feral cats. Maud was also almost blind in one eye, from an infection she had sustained too long before we got her, a fate we barely saved Ragnar from as well but that never hampered her in a long lifetime of bringing doom to the rats and mice in our barnyard. No one knows for sure why cats keep hunting even when they don't "need" to. Perhaps it is because in the wild, they may only catch prey in one try out of several?

A twelfth-century Norwegian translation of the Gospel of St. Nicodemus includes the word "mousetrap", rendered in Old Norse as "tréköttr", "wooden cat". The domestic cat probably only came to Scandinavia around the 4th-5th century CE at the earliest, but it quickly became the prototype for rodent control! The laws of early medieval Wales stated that in order for a settlement to be regarded as a full hamlet, it had to have nine buildings, one plough, one kiln, one churn, one bull, one cock, one herdsman...and one cat (van Vechten, p. 163).

In the wild they also cover meat and "save" it for later, so meat hunted early is like filling up the fridge. Also, there is evidence that cats see their territories the way people do their kitchens. Even if they are not eating some at the moment, they may be studying their cookbooks (or with cats, the habits of the local mice), only going to get the ingredients (hunting the mice) when they get their paycheck (the mouse is in position to be caught).

Whatever the reason – fish gotta swim, birds gotta fly, cats gotta hunt. Like human hunters, some are better at it than others. A few are super-hunters and a few are unable to catch anything at all. For the clueless non-hunter cat a responsible owner may want to consider a promising future as a house-pet, either in his own home or that of another household. The super-hunter cat is a cat worth her weight in gold, and a lot safer for everyone on your small holding than the amount of rat poison it takes to replace her.

It is also worth noticing that even if she a female super hunter is spayed, she may well teach unrelated kittens how to hunt, even adopting orphaned rescue kittens and showing them the ropes.

> When the Norse god Thórr, with his friend Loki and his servant Thjál-fi, went to the hall of the giant Útgardha-Loki, they had to face losing several apparently-embarrassing contests of prowess. At last, the giant said, "'Young lads here think it only play to lift my cat off the ground'... Then a gray cat sprang forth, and it was quite large. Thórr went over to it, put his hands beneath the middle of its body, and tried to lift it up. But the cat bent its back in just the degree that Thórr raised his hands, and when he had stretched as far as up as he could, the cat lifted one foot; and Thórr did not carry the game onwards..."

A humiliating moment for the god; or a very large, heavy, and reluctant cat indeed! But after Thórr has left the hall, his host reveals, "'All who saw (the cat-lifting) were frightened when they saw that it raised one of its feet from the ground, for that is not such a cat as you thought. It was in reality the Midhgardh-Serpent that encircles all lands...you raised it so high that your hands nearly reached to heaven'" (Snorri Sturluson, Prose Edda, Gylfaginning, 47-48 ; tr. Stephan Grundy).

Whether or not she adopts them outright, her influence will still serve as an example for them to follow. This is more likely if she has already had one litter of her own, which encourages her maternal instincts to operate even after she is spayed. Cats can improve their hunting skills, just as people can. It's not all inborn talent, it is also a practiced skill which is normally taught to kittens by older cats – usually a mother, elder sister, or neutered "uncle cat".

This also leads to the well-known kitty habit of delivering fresh-killed presents to the people. There are a couple of theories as to why cats do this. Perhaps it is an effort to teach us, big clumsy creatures that we are, the basics of Remedial Hunting; perhaps they merely want to contribute to the family food supply.

Tempting as it may be to express a certain degree of disgust at the appearance of the cat's little tasty treats on the doorstep or, god forbid, the bed (there are few things in normal household life not quite as charming as a deceased rodent lying bloodied on a white bedspread), it is important to remember that the cat is doing her job, and to praise and reward her while surreptitiously disposing of the offering. Freya, our rather psychotic Maine Coon, went from being a very clumsy hunter to a very effective one in record time when she discovered that showing up at the door or window with a dead mouse in her jaws was a sure-fire way to be invited in and given cat treats in return for the rodent.

CHAPTER 1: THE BASICS

FOOD & WATER
FEEDING CATS REGULAR MEALS

Basic feeding is a must. A full cat is a happy cat; a happy cat is a full-time hunter. Whatever you do - do not starve your barn cats in hopes that they will hunt better. It will simply slow them down and leave them open to illness and injury. Cats hunt for fun and emotional satisfaction with no additional motivation required, and a well-fed cat is a cat who can devote its full attention to catching and crunching its little squeaky toys. The myth that "a hungry cat catches more mice" is just that – a myth.

While hunting vermin is what first attracted cats to farms, the vermin alone are not really a sufficient diet for a modern cat colony. If they only have rats and mice to eat, their diet will be dependent on how good the hunting was that day. In the old days, cat populations would tend to go up or down accordingly. Hungry cats would fan out into nearby woods or pastures looking for tiny game, and some might even starve to death during a bad season. But the wonderful secret of cats is that they are born to hunt.

From the time they open their eyes, it's on their minds and all kitten play is practice for it. Cats don't need to be hungry to motivate hunting. In fact, they hunt much better on a full stomach (well, OK, maybe an hour after they get a full stomach). Like a human hunter who's had a good breakfast, they are more alert, less frantic, and focused on their prey, not on their hungry tummies. Cats, like other animals, need fresh water. On many farms they happily share this with the horses, dogs, chickens, etc., And use any other water source they can get to. But because cats are territorial, it's a good idea to give them their own water dish too. This is most important in either very warm or very cold weather.

In warm weather they can dehydrate quickly if the other water sources become scarce. In cold weather it's important to break the ice off the cats' water, just as you would for the horses, dogs and sheep. Most people think of both dogs and cats as meat eaters. But in reality dogs can eat a lot of different foods, whereas cats are "obligate carnivores". This means that they need mostly meat with tiny bits of other things added in. Since cats cannot conserve nitrogen as more omnivorous animals do, going too long without sufficient protein causes muscle breakdown (desperately cannibalizing the body's last protein resources for survival), liver failure and death.

A kitten requires half again as much protein for its weight as a puppy does. An adult cat requires two or three times as much protein for its weight as an adult dog does (an adult cat, etc., needs ca. 4 grams of protein/kilo of body weight/day. In contrast, humans who are not seriously training to build muscle require about .8 grams of protein/ kilo of body weight). Also, dogs evolved to frequently make large kills in groups, so that their metabolism is able to deal reasonably well with a very large meal followed by a period of starvation.

Cats are just the opposite: a huge feed will not sustain a cat's protein needs for too long, and if left with free access to food, will have between seven and twenty small meals/day by nature and choice (Hamper et AL, p. 237). This doesn't mean you have to feed your cats leftover steak every day. What it does mean is that food intended for cats should be slanted to a diet heavy on meat and lower on other foods.

The "Five Freedoms" are considered a basic benchmark for judging animal welfare of all sorts. They are:

1) Freedom from thirst, hunger, and malnutrition (having ready access to fresh water and a full and healthy diet).

2) Freedom from discomfort (suitable environment, including shelter and comfortable resting place, provided).

3). Freedom from pain, injury, and disease (by prevention and by rapid diagnosis/ treatment).

4) Freedom to express normal behavior (has plenty of space, proper facilities, and company of the animal's own kind).

5) Freedom from fear and distress (ensuring conditions that avoid mental suffering).

Cats can use some carbohydrates: their requirement is unknown, presumed low, but a bit of carbohydrate in the diet improves lactation and nursing-kitten support in queens, and probably aids health overall in cats. The easiest way to feed a barn cat colony is to buy a cheap brand of dry cat food in large bags at the feed store, and then add a few household leftovers.

The dry food bag should have suggested amounts per size of cat. You can just multiply the average amount by how many cats you have, subtracting some if you are adding leftovers to top up with. Adult cats are fine with once a day feedings, but young cats or elderly ones may need twice. A few brands of dog food also have a high enough meat content for cats (20% protein, if supplemented with other things, seems to serve well), but you must check with a vet for local information.

No cats should ever be fed on a diet of dry dog food alone as even the high protein brands lack some food elements that cats must have in order to be healthy. But you can mix it with dry cat food, and meaty table scraps, if your budget is tight.

Just remember that cats fed only on a diet of dog food can become ill or even die. Wet cat food and dry cat food are evenly matched in terms of nutritional qualities. Cats can thrive on either. A cat who has been raised exclusively on one may not be willing to eat the other; it does not do to give your barn cats a chance to become totally attached to one single type of food.

The only other issue with dry food as the primary food source is that cats normally have a low thirst drive (they are desert animals, who get some of their liquid from eating their prey in the wild), and cats who eat dry food only are at a higher risk of developing urinary stones and possibly other urinary difficulties due to low-level, chronic dehydration. If dry food is all you can manage for the cats, then at least soften it with some water if you can to lower this risk. Barn cats also enjoy left over family food, and, like people, do well with a varied diet. We make a point never, ever to give our barn cats bird bones (cooked or raw).

The cooked ones can splinter and choke them; raw chicken is so nice to a cat that identifying the smell and taste may incline the cat to go hunt its own supply – i.e., your laying hens. Fine fish-bones are also best avoided if possible, as again, there is a slight risk of lodgment in the cat's throat with disastrous results. But all other forms of leftover meat tend to go into the cat food dish. Most barn cats will also be happy to share family leftovers of other foods containing dairy or meat bits. Leftover mashed potatoes, oatmeal, or pancakes won't hurt them in moderation; but from a nutritional standpoint, are better left for the chickens.

In a food emergency, barn cats can be fed on things like leftover bread or rice soaked with gravy. This should only be done for a meal or two, but can be a lifesaver during severe weather or other crises. Raw meat is acceptable for cats, but it's safer for them (and, downstream, you) if it has been frozen to ensure an absence of parasites. If you butcher your own animals, the cats will be happy to "help" you with various leftovers.

However, you may want to check with your local vet or agricultural service concerning the safety of offal. Be careful not to give cats too much fat all at once, as it will just make them ill and incontinent. During very cold weather, working cats do need more food and fat, the same way that people do. An easy way to provide extra fat or protein is to pour leftover cooking oil or non-fat dry milk over their food. Eggs, raw or cooked, are also a good way to add extra nutrition.

But be careful to break up the eggs, otherwise you may find your barn cats deciding to collect the chicken eggs for themselves before you can get to the hen house! More chicken eggs are endangered by rats than felines, but it is easier to prevent bad habits than to break them once they start. If you really want to do homemade cat food, a combination of brown rice and de-boned cooked chicken can be used, along with top ups from other meat and carbohydrate sources.

Some of the most expensive dry cat foods are a combination of brown rice, plus chicken (or turkey) with cornmeal, flavorings and cat vitamin supplements. Some pet supply and feed store outlets even sell the vitamin powder to add to homemade cat blends. In nature, cats get their vitamin requirements from, variously, the vitamin and muscle tissue of their prey; and your working cat is likely to, at least occasionally, eat enough of her own kills to supply her needs.

THINGS TO WATCH FOR
- *LACK OF APPETITE*
- *INCREASE, DECREASE OR CHANGE IN POOP OR URINE*
- *CHANGES IN STRIDE (ALSO CALLED GAIT)*
- *CHANGES IN ACTIVITY: INCREASE IN SLEEPING, LACK OF SLEEP, UNABLE TO PLAY OR POUNCE*
- *GROOMING HABITS: LACK OF GROOMING, INCREASED GROOMING, MATTED FUR, LOSS OF FUR, CHANGES TO FUR*
- *SOCIABILITY: INCREASED HISSING, BITTING, INCREASED HIDING.*

Note that cats should not be fed an all- or predominantly-liver diet (or given excessive supplements), as, though more tolerant to vitamin A excess than humans or rodents, they still can suffer toxicity. Those who live in areas where fishing is an important part of the society and/or economy (or who just like to fish) need to be aware that, if the cats get fish on anything like a regular basis (and if you live in the right place, fish guts may be somewhere between 'real cheap' and 'free for haul away if you can stand the smell'), it needs to be fairly well-cooked.

The reason for this is that some raw fish contains enzymes which break down vitamin B1 (thiamine). Cats have a high requirement for dietary thiamine, roughly four times that of dogs: thiamine deficiency in cats (and other mammals) causes severe neurological consequences including anorexia, depression, staggering, dilated pupils, weakness, seizures, and ultimately death (Hamper et AL, p. 240). And thiamine deficiency absolutely can and does occur in every animal that needs thiamine and also eats too much raw thiaminase-containing[2] fish.

It's not a good idea to feed adult cats pure cow's milk, unless they have grown up drinking it. Tiny bits mixed in other food, or non-fat milk sprinkles on dry cat food are fine. But more than that is not a good idea. Like a lot of people, cats lose their ability to process milk after they are weaned, unless they continue to drink it every day.

2 Thiaminases are enzymes found in a few plants and the raw flesh and viscera of certain fish and shellfish

So, unless your barn cat drinks from the cow every day, Old Tom is better off with cultured dairy products like leftover cheese or yogurt. Goat milk is more easily digested by cats and better suited to their nutritional requirement than cow's milk, and can even be used for feeding nursing kittens in an emergency. Sick cats and nursing mothers can be given "cat milk".

This is milk that is sold in pet food aisles and is treated to prevent the diarrhea that untreated milk can cause – or else lactose-free milk, often available in grocery shops, since many humans are also lactose-intolerant. Special formulas designed for orphan kittens and puppies are also safe to feed young, pregnant, elderly or ill adult cats.

These formulas can often be purchased in powdered form for easy storage. And the powder can easily be added to homemade cat foods if needed. Some cats do get strange or unusual tastes in food, most of which are harmless and can be catered to in moderation. About one cat in ten goes absolutely crazy for corn cobs, and others will go nuts over lettuce and other greens. Outdoor cats naturally eat some greens, but it's a very tiny part of their diet. The most common cat food fetish seems to be cats who only eat dry cat food and nothing else.

Most of these are house cats, but it's something to look for if you choose to start your barn cats with cats from the animal shelter. Even then, it is only a problem if you plan to use only homemade or canned cat food. Otherwise, it's just a matter of making sure the cat in question gets some dry food every day and, as mentioned above, doing your best to make sure that it also gets all the liquid by mouth it needs to avoid later urinary problems. Feeding tiny kittens will be covered in the section on raising orphan kittens.

The easiest way to feed barn cat kittens after weaning is with commercial dry kitten chow. At about five to six weeks of age kittens will start to wean themselves and you can experiment by putting cat milk mixed with bits of wet or dry cat food on a very flat dish. They will walk into the dish and get very wet and very cute. But they will figure it out very fast. The main thing to remember is that young kittens need to eat more than once or twice a day.

So you may need to feed mother and babies extra feedings for a few weeks. If you practice cat birth control, this shouldn't be a problem very often. But almost all barn cat owners wind up with kittens once in a while, either from mother cats who wander off and are not spayed fast enough, or tiny kittens dropped on the doorstep by misguided humans who think that dumping kittens is kinder than taking them to an animal shelter. Most kittens dumped this way will die horribly beneath the wheels of cars or hunted down by larger animals. A few precious ones may be lucky enough to make it to your doorstep, where you can choose to take them in, or at least take them to the shelter yourself.

Cats are very conservative in their habits, the Tories and Republicans of the farm yard. Because they resist changes in routine, it's a good idea to feed them in the same spot every day. For barn cats, this usually means somewhere off the ground so the dogs and chickens don't get the food first. Large retired cook pots seem to work best for food dishes. Plastic can be used but tends to fall apart with long term use, and glass or pottery dishes break very easily. If you have more than three or four cats, be sure to use more than one dish.

This assures that everyone gets something to eat. If you have to change the cat feeding location, be prepared to listen to hostile meows from the old feeding place for a few days. But they will adjust to the new spot and soon be just as fond of it as the old one. The same conservatism is true for other issues of cat life such as sleeping shelters and the location of indoor cat boxes.

A fat cat will have the shape of an elongated ovoid with no waist visible (or just an ovoid, or possibly a sphere, depending on how fat the cat is). Again, be cautious in using sight alone to judge a long haired cat. Some can look like round fur pillows on visual inspection, but be nothing but skin and bones underneath.

The large gray cat of the Otherworld is still a familiar figure in Icelandic Júl (Yule) celebrations today, as the terrifying "Yule Cat", who comes about at Christmastime to devour anyone who has not received some article of new clothing...and who is commemorated in a huge LED-adorned statue in Reykjavík's city centre. The Yule Cat is sometimes presented in art as very thin and hungry, sometimes as exceedingly fat.

The jury is still out on whether the whole idea was invented by a grandmother who got tired of her family's lack of gratitude for home-knitted socks. Despite the Yule Cat, Icelanders love their cats. Many Icelandic cats are descended from the large longhairs brought west by Norse traders on the Eastern routes, but Icelanders import cats of all breeds.

There is a cat café in Reykjavík ("Kattakaffihúsið" – all cats are shelter cats and available for adoption), and a website entitled "Spottaði kött" ("Spotted a Cat!") devoted to cat pictures, many of which would be embarrassing if cats were embarrassed by that sort of thing. The popular Icelandic reality TV show, "Keeping up with the Kattarshians" is a live-action show following, basically, young shelter cats in a "dollhouse" designed for cat comfort, and is another vehicle for encouraging cat adoption (Nanna Gunnarsdóttir).

BIRTH CONTROL

Birth Control is vital for population control within your barn cat colony. On their own, cats do this by a combination of battles, infanticide, and starvation of weaker members. This is one case where "traditional" is definitely NOT the best practice. If money is tight, start by neutering your chief tomcat. He will still fight off predatory males and protect his females; he just won't make any more kittens.

Spay your females as time and finances permit. Many vets and animal charities provide discounted rates for people in need. Call them and explain your situation. Most farms only really need about five to eight barn cats. One mother cat and her children can create hundreds of kittens over a decade or two. If you are lucky, you will be able to start your own colony from scratch.

The easy way is to call around animal shelters (or farming friends) asking for a mother cat and kittens. Explain you are a smallholder who needs five or six cats, so they know you have space for them. You would be amazed how often mother and kitten combinations turn up in these places. Yes, many shelters require you to pay a deposit for vaccinations and altering. But you will really need to do that anyway.

A cat whose spine, ribs, and/or hipbones can be seen or are obtrusive to the touch; a cat with a constantly dishevelled or ruffled-looking coat...this is a cat who has something wrong with it, which could be anything from easily solved problems such as diet or parasite load to a fatal disease."vehicle for encouraging cat adoption (Nanna Gunnarsdóttir).

BASIC MEDICAL CARE

In an ideal world, all cats who were not meant to breed would be spayed or neutered; all cats would get all their vaccinations, regular treatment to prevent parasite infestations, and so forth. We do not live in an ideal world, and sometimes it is simply impossible in practical terms to do everything that we would choose to do if possible.

One fairly simple thing that can help maximize the effectiveness of any treatment that is more than a once-off (booster shots on vaccines, anti-parasitics, etc) is for someone in the household to keep a written record of what cats you have and note down the date and treatment whenever one of them requires medical attention, particularly things such as vaccine boosters.

Listing your cats is also a good idea for when you have to distribute a dose of medication to everyone in the colony, especially if there are several humans helping in the process: each cat's name is checked off for its dose by whoever got the medication down it, and that way you know that no one is either left out or double-treated. If an animal is in obvious pain or distress, it is absolutely time to intervene. You need to start by bringing the animal into shelter, usually your house.

If you have indoor cats, you need to use a room that can be isolated into a hospital area. Even if you have no indoor animals, a small room is best because sick cats will want to run and hide. Observation and isolation can help you determine if this is a home-treatable problem or a one that absolutely requires a vet. If you have a good relationship with your local vet, he or she may be willing to help do this sort of triage over the phone.

A rural vet understands why a busy farmer can't just rush out at midnight with a sick barn cat. In fact our local vet was astonished when we once insisted on doing so in an emergency (The call was actually for one of our house cats - a barn cat, suddenly severely ill at that hour, would probably have crawled off and died in the night, unless she had already been brought inside for observation). Many illnesses can be treated at home, or with one trip to the vet for a quick diagnosis and medicine.

Remember, money spent here helps protect the investment you've made in your other barn cats and livestock. While I have splinted a kitten's tiny leg with a Popsicle stick, I only did it after a city vet refused to accept time payments. Obviously a farmer or smallholder cannot afford radiation treatments for cancer or insulin for diabetic cats.

Vaccinations are usually given IM (intramuscular) or SC (subcutaneous). Your vet will tell you which to use with each type of injection. In cats, the easiest and safest place to do an intramuscular injection is in the thick muscle of the upper hind leg. SC injections in cats are normally given into a fold of loose skin at the back of the neck. Once the basic process has been demonstrated by a friendly vet or vet tech, the average person should have no problem doing either for their own cats. Anything involving IV injections, IV fluids, IV blood draws etc., should be left to those who have experience doing these procedure on cats. Even my husband, who is trained and experienced in doing such procedures on humans, refuses to give cats IV injections due to the differences in size and location between their blood vessels and those with which he is familiar. If you think this is a skill-set you may need, your best bet is probably to ask a friendly animal health-care professional for a tutorial.

Either condition, and many other severe conditions, may go unnoticed in a barn cat, who may not show signs of illness until the disease is quite advanced. The basic suggestions are to be observant; look out for major medical problems and deal with them as they occur; and keep up with the most essential maintenance procedures such as spaying/neutering and vaccination. Vaccinate as much as you can afford to do. A rural vet may be willing to show you how to vaccinate the cats yourself and sell you the injections.

If they know you are already injecting your own cows and sheep, why not the cats too? Ultimately his work load is lower if he can lessen infection rates around the county. Many people arrange to have the vet come out once a year and do everyone at once. It's still a lot cheaper than paying for an office visit (not to mention the logistics of getting those six to twenty cats to the vet's office), and we combine it with large livestock checkups when we can.

If doing it this way, be sure to contain all cats in a readily-accessible place before the vet arrives! Remember, like your plough horse and your sheep dog, these cats are WORKING animals, not just pets. Having their basic vaccinations (especially rabies) in the US, is not wasting money, it's protecting yourself and your livestock.

Beyond the diseases prevented by vaccination, barn cats are also vulnerable to injury and infection, particularly of the mouth and feet. If one of your cats is limping or seems to be having trouble eating dry food, take a look at it.

A strained leg or clean cut on the pad will usually heal by itself; an infected cut requires a trip to the vet – cats can die of blood poisoning or gangrene just like people can. If the cat cannot put any weight on its leg and cries when it is touched, it may have a broken bone, which also requires a trip to the vet.

If the cat's face appears distorted, the likeliest cause is either a serious dental infection or a broken facial bone. The former absolutely requires antibiotics; both are likely to require analgesia; and both are clear grounds for taking the cat to the vet.

> **Feeding Tips**

1. Choose a high quality food
*2. Feed according to your cat's weight. Use the guide
on the tin or bag to determine how much is too much
or too little.*
*3. Try to stay on schedule. Skipping meals is as bad for
cats as it is for people. Animals will get in the habit of
constantly overeating if they are not sure if or when
meals are arriving. Irregular mealtimes can also lead
to pushy behavior at mealtimes (feline or human),
fighting over food bowl access, and dedicated efforts to
steal human food.*
*4. Some cats overeat out of boredom. Try combating
this by presenting the food in a cat "puzzle dish" or
puzzle dispensing box, both readily available from
good pet stores or the Internet."*

Infected or broken teeth may have to be removed. This will not hinder the cat's hunting ability, as the claws are the primary means of catching prey. One cause of a distorted face that does not usually require a vet visit is a bee or wasp sting. Sometimes cats will try to eat these insects, and get stung on the face or inside the mouth. Remove the stinger if the cat will let you; the injury should otherwise resolve on its own. Finally, thick green or yellow mucus coming out of the nose and cruddy, weepy eyes must be dealt with by a course of antibiotics at once.

While cat upper respiratory infections are most often viral, it is common for cats to get severe bacterial infections on top of the initial virus. Antibiotics are normally given with these particular symptoms. If a case of cat flu is left untreated and the animal survives, it may remain chronically ill and be a walking reservoir of re-infection for all your other cats and any new ones that wander in. Such a cat (it will continue to sniffle, weep, and drip mucus weeks after it should have recovered) cannot be kept in a healthy barnyard: it must be re-homed as a permanent indoor pet (preferably where it cannot contact other cats) or, sadly, put down.

Cat flu is probably the biggest destroyer of cat colonies, and, if the cats have had their vaccinations, is the only problem that will linger to sicken and kill generation after generation if it is not dealt with thoroughly. Injury is often a gray area, when it comes to treating barn cats. They are pretty tough little creatures and can often recover if they are provided with warmth, food and comfort.

A vet really is needed to set broken bones or the aftereffects of car accidents. But if you are really close to the edge economically, and the choice seems to be letting nature take its course or just euthanizing the cat, you may choose to treat at home instead. Common injuries of this type are lost tails and infected abscesses.

> *"Observation and isolation can help you determine if your cat has a home-treatable problem or a one that absolutely requires a vet. If you have a good relationship with your local vet, he or she may be willing to help do this sort of triage over the phone."*

It's important to know that cats don't easily show pain, unless they are in complete agony. Nature has taught them to keep quiet or risk being killed by predators looking for an easy meal. Purring doesn't mean they are all right either, since even cats who are near death may purr. The one thing you can be sure of: if a cat is actively crying out in pain, it is in TERRIBLE pain, and it is very cruel to ignore it. More detailed information on common injuries and illness will be provided in the medical section (Chapter 5).

To sum up: treat at home what you can, call the vet when you must, but don't ignore illness and injuries in hopes they will go away. You are going to lose some barn cats anyway. Cats naturally go and hide when they are ill and come out if they live and don't if they die. Since their jobs require them to roam about your property, unlike housebound cats, you may not even realize they are gone until it's too late. Young kittens will get into situations they can't get out of, that's why cats produce four or five kittens at time.

When you can help, it's best to do so. By implementing the feeding/affection/birth control/vaccination system, you are already a long way towards keeping your family, your livestock and your barn cats healthy. If you follow these three basic items, your reward will be: a stable, non-feral, healthy barn cat colony of friendly working moggies (non-purebred cats to US readers), well fed and well "paid."

If you show them affection, you also get animals whose company you and your family can enjoy. This will also make retirement easier if a cat becomes too old or frail to "work" outside. An old, but friendly cat is much easier to retire to your own kitchen or that of a friend. A warm stove, a comfy basket and a catnip mouse are all great rewards for service well rendered, and even a "retired" cat will keep the mice out of the house, both by catching those it can and by frightening them away with the smell of cat.

➢*In addition to food, population control, and medical care, there are two things that are vital to keeping your cat colony at its best: proper shelter, and human affection.*

SHELTER

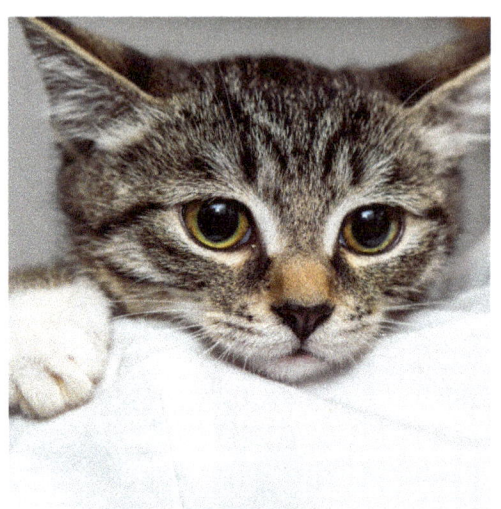

Shelter is important because cats need a warm, dry place to sleep when they are not busy decimating your rodent population. Good places are a barn with hayloft, any protected outbuilding, a dairy, or even a covered porch. Cat colonies will naturally tend to divide themselves into their own "territories" anyway. Just be careful that in very severe weather (bitter cold or snow) they have a warm place to gather.

In extreme cases, opening up the garage and inviting in the cats can be a good strategy. Other temporary shelters can be made from wooden crates or old boxes stuffed with worn out wool clothing. Because cats are small animals, providing cozy areas of warmth to snuggle in may be more effective than trying to heat a larger area. Cats that have good shelter will be less likely to become ill and more likely to recover quickly and completely. They will also be better-rested and hence more effective hunters. And many of the areas cats prefer for sleeping, such as haylofts, are places where vermin deterrence is most needed. While this topic is a lot simpler than feeding, it helps to understand how a cat sees his or her world. To a cat, territory can be even more important than their human friends.

Most cat lovers have stories about the cat that tried to get back to a former house when moved. The reason is the cat thinks they and their people are lost - after all no one would ever want to leave a good territory, would they? This is why, when you bring a new cat to your farm, you absolutely must lock it up somewhere for at least two weeks before letting it go free. A month is better. This can be anywhere from inside the house to a kennel cage (a secured outbuilding works well).

The new cat must have time to see, hear, and smell its new world long enough to settle in it. Young cats may do this in as little as a week, but moving a battle-scarred old warrior may take a month or more. But once a new territory is accepted, cats still have a few basic needs. Female cats, even spayed ones, will always look around for shelters that include soft, hidden places to hide kittens in safely and comfortably.

They may or may not be willing to share this space with sister females. In a larger group (five or more cats); females will almost always group themselves into two or more social groups and make mini territories of their own. This would be where they would hide their kittens if they had any. Each group will have several different hiding places because mother cats want to move litters often, in order to keep them safe. So for female cats the best shelter is often the hay barn, garage or other cluttered indoor area.

Some smallholders keep a cat door on an enclosed porch with boxes on it. This is a very good idea in areas with large predators like coyotes or pumas. Feeding the cats only on the porch will encourage them to use it. Male cats have a different view of the world. They don't want a mini-territory with warm snuggly places in it. They want the entire territory, control of all its females, dominion over all junior males, and warm snuggly places of their own, in it. In his mind, your Patriarch will be King of all he surveys and husband to all the other cats in it.

Even if he can never make kittens, he thinks he can and will behave accordingly. Junior males (beta toms) will be looked at as his teenage sons, even if they are older than he is. As long as they don't challenge him, he will tolerate them and let them share mini-territories with their "mothers and sisters" - even if the relationships are biological fictions and exist only in the minds of the cats. This is particularly the case if they were neutered before puberty (usually ca. 6 months): such a cat will always smell like a kitten to other cats, and receive considerably more tolerance from a King Tom.

Strange males are intruders and will usually be beaten off at all costs and his females may help him. In their minds the senior tom is the father of their future kittens. If the old leader loses, the new Tomcat is likely to kill any existing kittens in hopes of fathering his own, and to kill or drive off the junior males. An altered alpha tom keeps the barnyard quiet and stable. Stray females are more likely to be allowed to stay, and as the ultimate authority it is up to you to decide if they stay or go to the animal shelter.

There is another advantage to neutering your Tom. He will fight just as hard as a full Tom to keep his females and run off strange males, but he won't feel the urge to wander around to collect a bigger harem (thus getting into more fights and leaving the home turf undefended). Some neutered Tom cats will still wander but they tend not to go as far or as often. Toms neutered much after the age of six months are more likely to spray urine and go wandering. But even they tend to settle down somewhat after they have the operation.

The advantage of neutering a potential feline patriarch a little later (say, nine to twelve months) is that a tom neutered around six months will continue to act and smell like a kitten, whereas, if he has had the chance to become at least partially sexually mature and has the personality to be a dominant tom, losing his knackers will affect only his reproductive ability and tendency to leave the territory. A neutered tom or gib-cat[3] may continue to service unspayed females (or importune spayed ones on occasion). If he goes up in the barnyard hierarchy, he may start doing this even if he wasn't doing it before.

This is perfectly normal; it just means that his testosterone levels are increasing due to his new social status (if he goes all the way to the top, he is also likely to develop "'stud jowls' thickened lower cheeks, which may also disappear if the cat is neutered and slopes lazily down from or loses his place as barnyard King"). Some breeders

---

3 'Gib-cat' or 'gibbed tom' is an old-fashioned term for a neutered male cat, still used occasionally in rural Britain and Ireland

deliberately have a good-natured pet tomcat vasectomy rather than neutered as a special companion for their queens who are on heat, but not to be bred at the time.

Why are male cats called "toms"?

There is some question about how early the first recorded usage is – late mediaeval/early Renaissance have been suggested. However, it is generally believed that the common use of the term can be traced back to the mid-eighteenth-century book, The Life and Adventures of a Cat (Anon.; Variously attributed to Henry Fielding and/or William Guthrie; pub 1760).

This very popular work of its time recounts the many amorous adventures of a cat named Thomas; and Tom the male cat has remained in English to this day. Properly, a tom is an intact male and a neutered male is a gib-cat; but the cat is unaware of his actual fertility status, and it's probably best not to try explaining it to him.

Before The Life and Adventures of a Cat, whether "Tom" was in much use or not, it was more common to refer to the intact male cat as a "ram" or a "boar". The current domestic terms, however, have reached functional official status, to the point that "tom" and "queen" are terms that are applied formally to male and female tigers, lions, leopards, and other felines.

These boys can and will do everything the queen desperately wants them to, without little furry consequences nine weeks later. The downside is that they also will not act like gib-cats – because they aren't; they're still cranking out as much testosterone as ever, and as far as they know, every mating effort achieves everything they wanted it to. Neutered toms, both your Patriarch and his junior flunkies, are likely to live much longer than their intact brothers, because they do not wander about, they are less likely to be hit by cars - the most frequent eliminator of domestic cats, at least in the industrialized world.

So you won't need nearly as many cats as you would in a feral, unregulated colony. In brief: cats do need some shelter but the average set of farm buildings is perfect for them. Haylofts are among the best places, followed by workshops, sheltered porches, stables etc.

In severely cold weather (about 10 degrees below freezing) they must be brought inside, or they can freeze to death. Any sheltered building will do, but a heated area is even better. In very hot weather cats need shade as well as plenty of water. They are pretty good at finding shady spots on their own, without help from humans.

The Danes were not the only people who saw the farm cat as embodying the luck of the household. In parts of Germany, the house "kobolt" (a term also applied to earth elementals and mine-spirits, but here, a being rather like the Swedish tomte or Scots brownie, responsible for the household's well-being) may have appeared as a tomcat or cat-man (Grimm, II, ch. 17). Such beings must be treated well, lest they leave and take the home's prosperity with them.

AFFECTION

It's possible to domesticate adult feral cats. I know, because I've done it. But it's a very long and tedious process that most farmers won't have time for. However, almost anyone can tame feral cats. That's because almost anyone can feed them every day, talk softly while putting down their food bowls, and allow them to feel safe enough to come near. As the weeks go by, some of the cats will become braver and will walk right up to their food source to express their gratitude by rubbing and purring.

A few more will ask to be petted and be happy to have their new friend sit down after dinner. If there are kittens, they will often be the first to investigate the large animal on two legs, even if their mother runs behind the hay bale. It's worth doing this, even if you have just inherited the scruffiest, mangiest barn cats you have ever seen, because many of them will come to love you, and cats who love you (even if you only like them) will be easier to catch and treat for illness, injuries, and birth control operations. Over time the health and size of your colony will become more manageable, and healthier, happier cats means better vermin control.

Cats need a SAFE place to sleep. It is not important what brand you buy or what type of bedding you provide, as long as it meets the needs of keeping your cat warm, happy, safe, and comfortable.

Children are useful to help fully domesticate formally feral barn kittens. Older children, that is: below the age of seven they are too likely to get hurt or hurt the kittens. But kittens love to play, and sense a kinship with human "kittens." If you don't have any human kittens around, you can imitate them by pulling strings, tossing tiny balls, and playing other games to lure hesitant kittens.

Being hunters, they will almost always follow a string, which you can pull closer and closer to yourself. After while they will leap on you (or your child) and then you can begin to pet them. Let the kitten (or older cat) tell you how much attention it can handle at first. The same techniques work for older cats, except they tend to be much more nervous and taming them is better left to patient adults or teenagers.

Old Irish laws mentioned "the very noble things which remove decline from little children, i.e. hurleys and balls and loops, or cats" and "the small playthings which someone begins with, i.e. small dogs and cats" as the legitimate possessions of childhood with specific legal protections and degrees of restitution (Murray, pp. 153-54).

Cats are more likely to do real damage if they are frightened. A mother cat will watch her kittens if children are playing with them and call them away if it upsets her. Again, children must be old enough to understand that they have to allow this to happen before they become junior "Cat Whisperers." But it's a great way for children to learn empathy with animals, enjoy themselves and do a useful farm job; all at the same time.

Children can also learn to feed the cats, but if you have a large number of cats you will want to make sure the child is not over-whelmed by the experience, not to mention, monitoring them to make sure the cats are fed each and every day. To sum up: cats treated with love and affection become loving and affectionate cats. Cats who are ignored and untouched become wild, nervous and difficult to approach.

Tame cats are easier to treat when ill or injured, and easier to catch for altering. They are less likely to accidentally injure a human by scratching or biting and they hunt as well as, or better than, cats who are afraid of people. Fully domesticated cats can provide humans with joy, entertainment, and love as well as being working partners.

Birth Control

When I first bring up the subject of spaying/neutering barn cats, many people ask me, *"Why bother? The cat population seems to stay about the same anyway."* This may even be partially true, especially near busy roads or large cat-eating predators. People also say, *"It's a system that has worked for centuries, so why interfere with it?"* There are several reasons why. In this instance, the old way may not be the best way, and it certainly isn't the kindest way. To understand why this is the case, we have to go back to some of the previous information on how cats view their world.

We have already talked about how cats perceive the world in terms of their territories. From a barn cat's view point, she owns her mini-territories and rights to its food supply. Tom owns all the females and his friends on your entire farm. I know it may feel strange to be "owned" by cats, but this is how they look at things, not how humans see them. When new kittens are born, their mothers will do everything they can to protect them.

Often this means pairing up and raising kittens together. One mother may even turn her kittens almost entirely over to her nursing sister to baby-sit and do hunting for two. I've always thought of this as the Artemis (Greek Hunting Goddess) and Demeter (Greek Mother Goddess) arrangement. But ultimately each female needs enough psychological space and food supply for herself and her kittens.

The Norse of the Viking Age and early medieval period were well-familiar with the reproductive enthusiasm of cats. The accuracy of the medieval writer Snorri Sturluson's claim that the wagon of the goddess Freyja (notable, among other things, for her sexual freedom) is drawn by two cats has been disputed.

However, there are several archaeological finds which suggest a likely linkage between felines and the goddess, including the repeated use of feline imagery on some of the probably-ritual and certainly-royal vehicles buried with the 9th-century Norwegian Oseberg women (often presumed to be "Queen Asa" and her handmaiden, though there is no way to tell which of the women was which).

In the "First Lay of Helgi Hunding's-Bane", the heroine Sigrún says scornfully of her unwanted betrothed that he is "shameless as a cat's son" (18) – which suggests a lot about his courting style. A Viking Age man of the Icelandic Settlement period, one Thórðr Thórðarson, bore the by-name "Tomcat".

The reason for this is never given, but it is quite possible that it meant just what it would today. The potential ferocity of cats was also recognized by the Viking Age Norse. According to Vatnsdoela saga (ch. 28), the Icelandic wizard Thorólfr Sledge kept a pack of large black cats as guardians; and his cat pack was quite sufficient to put the wind up a troop of armed and armored Norsemen.

Compared to people, cats mature very quickly, so in the wild, it is in the mother cat's best interest to encourage her youngsters to go off and find their own territories as quickly as possible. The more cats (and less food resources) there are, the faster this tends to happen. Some of her daughters may continue to live with her, but only if they can either share a mini territory with mom, or find their own nearby. Sons will be forced to strike out on their own pretty early.

Compared to people, cats mature very quickly, so in the wild, it is in the mother cat's best interest to encourage her youngsters to go off and find their own territories as quickly as possible. The more cats (and less food resources) there are, the faster this tends to happen. Some of her daughters may continue to live with her, but only if they can either share a mini territory with mom, or find their own nearby.

Sons will be forced to strike out on their own pretty early. If mom doesn't insist on this, their father will when they reach sexual maturity, somewhere between seven months and one year of age. Obviously cats that young and inexperienced are going to have a pretty high mortality rate when they go wandering. This is one of the ways nature ensures a balanced population of wild cats. Good for nature, perhaps, but very harsh for the young cat trying to find his place in the world. Then there is that lucky guy, the KING of every barnyard.

He's the winner of many battles and may very well have lost an eye or an ear to show for it. His job is to keep his kingdom free of all those young males who are wandering around from last year. His own sons, he may tolerate for up to two years if the game is good and he's in a good mood. When they get big enough to challenge him or he sees them sneaking off with their aunts, their time is up. Unless the King himself has grown old or weak; then his own son may win his crown and take his place.

This is rare, and biologically not a good idea, because the temporary nature of the Tom is what helps keep down inbreeding in the same group. And any good farmer knows what happens when animals get too inbred. Nature seems to recognize this and has several ways of dealing with it. However, one day our King will either be challenged by a younger Tom and driven off, probably to spend his last days eking out a living at the edge of his old territory - hunting solo if he is wild, or sneaking up to the food dish late at night if he's a barn cat.

Unless he finds shelter in another farmyard or territory, his life is likely to be very brief. Often he dies of the terrible wounds cats can inflict upon each other during the serious fights over ownership of their kingdoms. These are very different from most cat fights, which are just the Old Monarch running off a low-status and frightened stranger. Fights that run off other cats may sound terrifying at 3 AM, but most often the newcomer backs off and runs away after a brief exchange.

Participating cats can still get hurt, but it isn't usually the tearing open of stomachs and other fatal strategies used during a true Challenge for Kingship. It isn't adaptive to have males fighting to the death every other day, and cats are cautious by nature, and programmed to flee danger rather than confront it. Once in a while it happens, and to The Victor Go The Spoils. Now let's suppose we have a New Prince taking over his kingdom.

Many animals in the barnyard become restless. They, unlike the humans, know that something is going on. The dogs may bark and whine, the chickens are restless, and the female cats are oddly silent and have likely disappeared. An observant farmer may notice that Old Tom isn't around that morning, but that's not unusual since he often goes off to visit girlfriends at a nearby barnyard (toms will also sneak at night into each others' territories, and attempt to impregnate each other's wives behind their back).

What is strange is that some of the female cats are not coming out for breakfast, and there are no kittens to be seen, anywhere. The busy farmer puts food down anyway and goes on to do his other chores. Over the next few days he may notice that his Old Tom seems to have gone away for good and that there's another cat, New Tom, who has taken his place. He's still puzzled by the sudden lack of kittens. Then, barn cats have a high mortality rate and he doesn't usually pay that much attention anyway.

Soon, his sleep will be disrupted (if it hasn't been already) by the yowling of "cats making more cats," but that will subside in a few days' time. In about a month, he will notice that almost all the female cats are growing larger, even if it's an unusual time of year for mating. In two months he may be almost overrun with kittens. A new cycle starts all over again. What he doesn't see (usually) is the holocaust of kitten death that follows the disappearance of Old Tom. It's common folk knowledge that tomcats can be dangerous to small kittens. It's not true that they always kill kittens. Usually they only deliberately kill kittens they believe are fathered by another tom.

Just like lions on a T.V. Documentary, a new barnyard king will search out and find any kitten he can and destroy them mercilessly. Their mothers will go to great lengths to try and save them, moving them about from nest to nest, each next one higher and further away than the last. She can only move one kitten at a time. Almost always, this is her downfall: the tom will watch her when she moves and kill the kittens left behind. Once in a great while, a brave mother cat will manage to save one or two tiny kittens by taking them off into the bush.

44

Another may also be able to lead older kittens to safety in the same way. In either case she must raise them on her own hunting skills alone and hide them from other predators, all without the protection of the guardian tom and her sister- friends. If she is very lucky she may be able to return to the barn yard in a few months, mostly grown kittens in tow. It's more likely that she and they will move to another territory altogether and restart their family somewhere else - lost to their original barnyard, along with their hunting skills. Except for such rare escapes, all remaining kittens are usually murdered pretty quickly. This forces the grieving mothers to go into season.

It's not that they are heartless hussies as some people have suggested; anyone who has been around female mammals knows that maternal grief is not the sole province of human beings. The world of a cat is not the same as the human world. Even as they cry out with rage, their bodies understand that their kittens are gone forever and that they must replace them as soon as possible. Going into season also helps them establish bonds with New Tom, a stranger, whom they would otherwise avoid. Rapidly he sets up his new kingdom and tries to make as many kittens as possible. It's important for him to be quick about it.

Most Barnyard Kings only last for a few years; even one year is fairly common. So he must make his kittens early and often, if his genes are to have a chance to continue. Not all the kittens born in his kingdom are really his biological offspring. Just as he will go courting to nearby farmyards, other toms will do the same to him. And a few of the beta toms (adolescent or smaller males who hang about on the fringes of a dominant male's territory) will surely lure a lady friend off into the bushes as well.

Enough of the kittens are his own offspring that it makes biological sense for him to guard them and their mothers. While it's not a good idea to deliberately test a tomcat's love for his children by putting them in a small space together, as an owner you are likely to see touching scenes of daddy barn-cats washing and playing with their young kittens. Sometimes they may even babysit while mom is away. This is only because they are his own offspring, or he believes them to be. Mother cats are generally wary of letting tiny kittens near any barn cat tom, father or not, at least until the kittens are old enough to be scampering away if he's in a bad mood.

In addition to regular bouts of genocide by males, barn cat populations are naturally controlled by high mortality of young kittens and disease epidemics that carry off both young and old. Many farm kittens get eaten by farm dogs, fall into watering troughs or rain barrels, get stepped on by big feet (human and livestock), sleep inside the wrong tractor wheel, or just wander away and get lost and unable to defend themselves. There's not much anyone can do about this first problem, except lock up mother cats about to give birth and keep them inside until the kittens are older (we do this, but many people can't).

While you can choose to try and lock up mothers and vulnerable infants, there's not much you can do about disease, except provide as much care as possible (see next section). However, having a self-regulating "natural" population of barn cats almost insures that an epidemic WILL happen sooner or later. The reason is because a self-regulating population, especially one that is expected to feed itself only by hunting, is going to have huge differences in status and nutrition.

When I was a child we lived in a rural area of California where people were always dumping cats off near our hay stack. We did what we could but they were not really "our" cats and we couldn't afford to spay and neuter them all. My mother would buy huge bags of generic food (all we could afford) or mix up corn meal with milk to feed them. There were always some cats that looked very well and some that were literally starving.

Darwin is not always a pretty sight, especially when it's a tiny, crying, starved kitten. About every three years an epidemic of disease would sweep through, starting with the weaker cats and spreading quickly to the others. Our house cats were not spared and large vet bills and pitiful cardboard boxes buried in the back yard would fill our lives for about three weeks. When it was over, most of the outdoor cats would be gone, until more people started dumping more cats and the cycle would start all over again.

If we'd had a real working farm (like our neighbors) this cycle could have been more than just heartbreaking. It could have been extremely dangerous as well, since some diseases carried by cats can also affect other livestock or even human beings. Controlling the size of your barn cat population can't guarantee a disease-free barnyard, but it makes it a whole lot less likely. Your cats will be better fed and less emotionally stressed by territorial takeovers and, if you have fewer of them, it's a lot easier to afford to vaccinate or treat illnesses as they occur. Catching and dealing with seven cats is a lot easier than with thirty or forty of them.

Most farms or small holdings only need between five and fifteen cats. If you have a very large farm, with several sets of buildings, you may have to have several mini-sets of cats for each area. The cats themselves will probably arrange this anyway. Five to seven cats can pretty well manage a house and nearby barn complex on their own - maybe up to eight or nine if you have large stables and outbuildings. So, having now taken a trip through nature's way of dealing with cat populations, we can talk about The Happy Barn Cat way. This is simply Birth Control and as much of it as you can put in place.

This is much easier if you are able to start from scratch with your own chosen cats. It's harder (and more expensive) to begin to enforce it on an existing cat colony. It's worth it, even if you have to implement it in stages over time. The ultimate goal is having every single cat in your colony spayed and neutered. A cat that has been de-sexed is actually more likely to concentrate on the serious business (and sport) of hunting, and will certainly make a better pet.

If you live in a very dangerous area, enough to have a very high cat turn over, you spay and neuter everyone but your best mother and huntress. Even then, you will probably want to talk to your vet about putting her on the "Kitty Pill" part of the time. This is widely used for cat birth control in Europe and is sometimes used in the US by pedigreed cat breeders. And it's the ONLY way to keep Tiddles from finding a tom cat and arranging her own mating.

Female cats can breed up to 3x per year. On average, a female cat can have up to 4 kittens per litter. Population can explode and create a complete kitten crisis, resulting in increase pressure on shelters. The total number of cats estimated to descend from a single female over four years has been calculated to a staggering 2,107 cats.

An unspayed outdoor female cat is a mother cat, often several times a year. Unlike dogs, an unspayed queen will go into heat until she has bred, then do it again as soon as her litter is six or eight weeks old – over and over, until she is worn out or dies from a complication of breeding. It can be difficult to keep even a well-nourished, carefully-tended, purebred breeding queen from suffering vaginal and/or urinary infections in the course of her heats. If your hunting females are spayed, they are less likely to go roaming when they go on heat and risk being killed by cars or dogs.

They will not attract strange toms to fight with your present cats, nor will they run the risk of dying in birthing or from pre-birth complications. Kittens can get stuck inside just as human babies can, with fatal results to both infant and mother unless prompt intervention occurs: my husband has, several times, had to gently pull a kitten free of the womb in order to save the lives of mother and kit. Nor will they leave the barnyard to save their kittens or search out new territories because things are getting too crowded, which means that instead of one or two years' service out of a champion mouser, you may get ten years or longer.

The same is true for the Barnyard King, but even more so. An intact tom who is allowed outdoors will roam up to ten miles in search of females on heat, exposing himself to dangers from cars, dogs, and, not least, other tomcats. His chances of living to a comfortable old age are almost nil. A late-neutered King will still fight to run off strange toms, but he will not go out looking for trouble. In contrast to the one to four or five years that an intact Barnyard King normally lasts, our own cat-ruler, Prince Mordred, remained in excellent health and strength nearly all his life, lived to be sixteen, and died peacefully in his warm bed in the house.

If you feel you really need to "home grow" your own cats, you can take your number one huntress off the pill and let her have a litter or two. Then it's best to spay her and repeat the process with one of her daughters. Even better is to spay her and get future kittens from the local animal shelter. This is because a queen who has raised her own kittens and taught them to hunt will most often continue to teach any new kittens that are added to the group. She may not adopt them, or even seem to like them very much.

But she will show them by example and may even bring small animals for them to practice on, the same way she may leave "presents" for you to step on outside the door in the morning, because she knows you're a pathetic hunter and wants to help you practice the art. That's the main story about kitty sex and birth control.

Starting or Maintaining a Cat Colony

Not everyone gets to start from scratch. In fact, most farmers and smallholders are likely to acquire a barn cat colony along with the farm. The first step here is taming them (if they are semi-wild) enough to get near them. Then start paying attention to see if any are obviously sick or injured. This is where you may have to make some tough choices. The ideal solution is to find a local vet or veterinary college with a big heart (or students to teach) and ask for help. Explain that you inherited this situation and you want to deal with it in a humane manner (show them this book if you want).

You do need some barn cats, but you don't have any way to know which of the sick ones can recover and you certainly can't afford to alter twenty cats. At least not at full price, or not all at once. Contact the local S.P.C.A. as well, and ask for advice. Sometimes you will get lucky and live in an area where there's some charitable funding to help with these situations. You will get a vet who is willing to donate time (or use a sliding scale) to help out. Other places have local volunteer groups that help with feral cat populations. Don't be afraid to look at any and all sources of help and funding. Because what really needs to happen is three things:

1. Find some way to treat or humanely euthanize the sick and infectious cat.
2. Spay and neuter any cats you choose to keep.
3. Vaccinate them with basic vaccinations.

This last one may have to wait for the other two, but the other two need to happen as soon as possible. If you can't get any help (and sadly that's all too common), you will need to do this process by yourself. I don't mean castrate cats on your kitchen table, but start by doing what you can, as you can. First deal with the sick cats, they can be a danger to you and your other animals.

Most barn cats have runny eyes and the occasional runny nose, but if this is accompanied by deep coughing sounds, loss of weight, obvious diarrhea, etc. It's a sign of cat flu or other serious illness. Most cats recover, but if some of your cats just stay this way for weeks, they either need to be treated with antibiotics, re-homed or humanely put down for the sake of the rest of them. Yes, it's treatable, but there is no real cure for chronic cat flu.

I've managed to re-home several cats with this (and other) chronic problems as beloved house pets with people who can lavish medicine and care on them. I always explain first that the cat is **ILL**: that's why it needs a new home. Most smallholders and farmers don't have the time or the money to treat constantly ill cats. Triaging the members of an existing cat colony is likely to be the hardest and saddest part of your barn cat adventure, but it really needs to be done. If possible, call out the vet at least once to help you make the decisions. Something that looks medically serious may not be and something that doesn't appear to be a problem just might.

Remember, you DID NOT create this sad situation, you are trying to remedy it. Even if it developed on your watch, you didn't know any better, and now you do. Either way, you want to make things right as soon as possible. For obvious reasons, it is best to have the vet come out on a day when your children are not at home; culling sick animals is a hard enough job for trained adults to face. Better to let them help with the kitties who will need them afterwards - the ones the vets declare are able to recover. Now that we know your remaining cats are basically well, or recovering nicely, it becomes a matter of sterilizing them one (or two) at a time, as you can afford it.

Many vets and charitable organizations sponsor "spay and neutering drives" during which heavy discounts are offered to treat the animals. Even in rural Ireland you can get cats (and dogs) done very cheaply during the month of October. The local SPCA helps raise money all year to fund it. As you take each animal in (even if it's one every six months) try and get them their most important vaccinations too. If you cannot afford much in the way of vaccinations; explain the situation to your vet or SPCA and ask which medical procedures are the most critical; to protect both yourself and your livestock.

Remember that a working cat is not the same as a pet cat. Rural vets are more likely to understand this than city vets trained to work with house cats. The latter often have a view that "if you can't afford it, you shouldn't have the animal." "It" may be a whole series of very expensive and time-consuming procedures. Trained to a "best practice standard" for house-pets, they may not realize that in a rural area, you are likely to have the animals about anyway, for the reasons provided in the previous section. There will always be some barn cats hanging about the place; you are choosing to try to provide them as good a life as you can.

The last time I encountered this argument, that I should not have any barn cats unless I could afford every and all suggested medical procedure for every single barn cat, I was tempted to ask the urban vet in question, *"So, should I ask my husband to shoot them all instead?"* I'd never do that of course; I love all my animals (pets and barn cats alike) far too much to even joke about it. But that is the "other" solution to the problem. Since cats can be useful partners for farmer and small holder, it seems like a bitter and tragic waste, unless there is no other choice to prevent suffering.

To sum up: anything you can do is better than nothing. Start with spaying females, if you can. They are the ones making the kittens. If you are fond of Old Tom, do him early in the game, so you don't lose him. He will still think all the kittens are his. There are farms that use this system by itself to create stable barnyards and slow down the number of kittens. (Thomas, p. 94). As mentioned, your unspayed queens will still find unsuitable boyfriends when driven by nature. So try to take them to the vet one at a time.

Cats are less likely to breed in fall and winter (hence October here is discount altering month). So this is a good time to aim for. It's possible to spay a queen who is already pregnant. But it's harder on both cats and vets to do this. It can also be a more expensive operation. The ideal way to start a barn cat colony is to go to a local animal shelter (or nearby farm) and get a new mother and all her kittens. It's amazing how many mother-kitten units (and pregnant females) get dropped off at shelters, and if you let them know you are looking (and that you have a farm and have room for them) you are likely to get a phone call pretty fast.

Many shelters now require that animals be altered and vaccinated before they adopted, and that's just fine. It may cost a bit more than a "free" cat, but if you are running a farm, you can look at it as an investment in property protection. Vaccinated cats are the safest cats on a farm. The reason a mother-kitten unit is the best starting point is because the mother will care for them and teach her children hunting skills. If her children are neutered and spayed, she will never reject them. Her sons will live with her for life, although one is likely to proclaim his farmyard dominance over the barnyard. His brothers will allow this because they are related. And he in turn will not run them off for the same reasons.

Also, his testosterone levels won't be nearly as high as a full Tom's. He's got enough to secure his land from invaders, but not enough to go looking for trouble, at home or abroad. You can also do this with just a litter of kittens or unrelated cats young enough to adopt each other (below six months of age).

But unless you have an adult female who hunts, they may take longer to become good hunters themselves. Most cats can (and will) teach themselves to hunt. But they are quicker at it if they have some help.

Starting with a pregnant cat or mother/litter grouping also gives you the opportunity to raise the kittens to be affectionate companions, whom you can easily catch when you need to take them to the vet or give them medication.

Chapter 2: Taming the Feral Cat

To tame a feral cat, you have to start by understanding how the cat thinks. Cats in the wild (whether country or city) are in an unusual position: they are predators to most things their size or smaller, but they are also the prey of larger animals and things: dogs, some humans, cars and other machinery; in the countryside, coyotes and other wild animals; and, often enough, other cats. To survive, the cat in the wild must be continually alert, ready to attack at any moment in order to eat, but also ready to flee at any moment in order not to be eaten. The unknown is an endless threat: better to miss a meal than to die.

The cat buries her spoor in order to keep larger predators from detecting her presence; she hides her kittens as best she can when a strange tom comes in to do battle for the territory, because she knows that if he wins, he will kill her kits when he finds them; and when she is sick or injured, she hides until she dies or recovers, because to be caught in a weakened state is certain death. As a human, you are primarily a potential threat to her life. She has no way of knowing that you want to befriend her, until you have proven your safety over a long period of time.

When taming a feral cat of any age, the most important things to maintain are gentleness, patience, and regular contact. Avoid sudden movements; do not try to grab the cat. Food and play (the mouse-on-a-string is favorite) are the best way to lure a wild cat slowly towards you. Eventually, it will realize that it has been getting very close to you and is still unmolested. Some cats will, after a period of this treatment, allow you to pet them and pick them up. For a particularly wary cat that you want to rescue, you may need to use a humane trap to catch it.

Some feral cats domesticate themselves very completely when they realize that there are benefits such as nice food in it for them. Others will never be domesticated; the best you can do is see that cats like this have access to food, water, shelter, and whatever basic medical care you can manage to give them. `If it is possible to catch the cat and for you to keep it inside, it should be kept completely indoors for the first several weeks. Not only does this accustom it to human company, but it gives you a chance to restore it to full health.

A feral cat is almost certain to suffer from worms, which it gets from fleas and from eating mice, rats, and large bugs. Actually, any cat that eats its prey or comes into contact with fleas will need occasional worming: my husband recounted to me his horror at the age of fourteen when his purebred, exclusively house-dwelling sable Burmese T'Pau demonstrated to him just how visible a white tapeworm is against dark brown fur.

The cat was on his pillow at the time. She had contracted the unfortunate condition from eating bugs. As well as worms, feral and outdoor cats regularly have endemic cat flu (thick opaque mucus streams from the nose, snuffles a lot), infected eyes (often from the cat flu spreading, often from injury), boils and patches of infection (from accidents, from other cats' claws or teeth, or from rodent bites) which may stay localized or go septic or gangrenous and kill the cat, and a variety of other conditions.

The majority of these are potentially fatal to a cat if untreated. Some, such as cat flu, can wipe out a whole cat colony, but most are easily cured with a simple course of medication combined with good food and cleanly conditions. A trip to the vet is always one of the first orders of business once the cat has calmed down a little and realized that you aren't going to eat it. This is particularly important with females, as if a pregnancy is caught early enough, it is still possible to spay the cat without undue harm or trauma to her. If you have a female in late pregnancy.

You are going to have kittens; all you can do is provide good nutrition and medical care to make sure that she and her kits make it through as well as possible. A newly-caught feral cat should be kept in a room that has good hiding places in order for it to feel secure. It will probably stay mostly in hiding for anything from two days to a month. At this point, it is all right for you to reach in and pet it to help the cat get over its fear. Luring it out with a string-toy (the popular sport of cat-fishing) will also be quite helpful. Fortunately, because the instinct to bury its spoor is so strong, litter-training even a completely wild cat is a very simple operation.

All you need to do is scratch the cat's front paws in the litter so that it knows where it can do its duty. In fact, feral cats are often better than house-raised cats about this. We have had several house-raised cats who looked on a well-chosen (from the cat's point of view) location to widdle as an opportunity to express their annoyance, but a cat who has lived as prey in the wild always wants to bury the telltale leavings down where no other predator can smell that she had been there.

The exception to this is a mature tom, and by mature, we mean over six or seven months. Once a young tom has started spraying, neutering will not stop it. Old Lord of the Barnyard, Prince Mordred, was neutered a little too late (my husband's Forest Cat stud tom was a rare non-sprayer, so he didn't realize how much trouble an intact male could be until Mordred began to mark his territory).

Until he reached the age where his health necessitated a full-time household retirement, we couldn't let him in the house for more than a few minutes (for his retirement, we set him up in a room that was easily cleaned). Mordred's spraying, backed up by a tomcat's urge to fight for his territory, has helped keep strange cats out of our barnyard, but at the cost of his chances to be a part-time indoor pet for most of his life.

He was still immensely affectionate in his outdoor kingdom, and I have often seen my husband doing things in the yard with Mordred draped around his neck like a big tabby-striped scarf. Essentially, when choosing the time to neuter a young male, you must decide whether you want a Lord of the Barnyard or whether you want a perpetual kitten. A tomcat neutered before he starts showing signs of maturity will always smell, and act, like a kitten.

He will not challenge older toms for territory, and in turn is more likely to be accepted as a subordinate; he will not spray; and he will readily and always see humans as parental figures. A male cat snipped at or before six months usually makes the most affectionate and devoted pet of any cat, precisely because he will be a kitten psychologically (and in many ways hormonally) all his life. Neutered toms, even late-neutered, are much more inclined to be gentle with kittens and even teach them to hunt.

I once saw Prince Mordred engaged in a game of mousie-soccer with a recently adopted kitten, showing her what to do; and another of our late-neutered males (a Forest Cat who had turned out to be unsuitable for breeding) taught a kitten from a non-hunting mother to be a deadly hunter. Whether you want a pet or a working cat, it is always best to spay or neuter it. Cats do not necessarily become fat and lazy after being de-sexed, so long as they have active lives: our best mousers have all been snipped early. The main difference is that the cat will live longer and be healthier.

If you cannot actually bring your feral cat inside for any real length of time (though you will have to keep it in for a week or so to recover from its operation after neutering), the only way to tame it is through constant, regular contact. Cats are creatures of habit; "little furry Republicans with an inbuilt aversion to change" (S.M. Stirling, *Dies the Fire*). If you are the daily bringer of nice food, who lingers and speaks sweetly and gently to the cat without threatening it in any way or invading its personal space, eventually it will come to think well of you.

Cats are fundamentally social and affectionate creatures, but a feral one must be allowed to make the first move. Food is the most certain way to establish the link. Most people have seen cats rubbing up against their owners' ankles and purring when the can-opener comes out. What fewer realize is that this is the same submissive behavior shown by a kitten to its mother towards the end of the weaning process. When the cat rubs against you and purrs in hopes of being fed, it has established the transfer between mother-as-source-of-food/affection and human-as-source-of-food/affection.

We got a very good first-hand demonstration of how a maternally-socialized feral kitten initiates the bonding process, in contrast to a human-raised kitten, when we brought Ragnar, Siggi, and Svarti – the three kittens in the sidebar-story above -into the room with an old spayed female, Ostara. Siggi and Svarti, raised by humans, pounced on her constantly with no manners and were continuously cuffed aside, but Ragnar, raised by a mama cat, carefully rubbed up against Ostara, paused a moment to see if she would hit him or growl at him, then rubbed closer until she let him cuddle against her tummy and sleep with her.

A feral cat who is ready to be tamed will initiate and carry out this same slow and careful process with humans in just the same manner as a kitten approaches a strange older cat. In the country or in the city, the best way to tame a feral cat is to catch it when it's fairly young. The younger the cat, the more willing it is to accept human beings as substitute mothers – large warm animals that it can cuddle up next to for petting and depend on for food.

A feral kitten that was weaned early may actually develop the habit of nursing on its chosen human: my husband's first kitten, a frightened little refugee from the Humane Society, was inclined to suckle on the neck of his pajamas, purring and kneading constantly – even when she had grown to a huge (twenty-five pound) adult. The taming of Ragnar was what we would describe as an ideal situation for converting a feral cat into a working pet: he was young enough to readily transfer his affection to humans, but had already been taught to hunt very effectively by a wild mother.

In addition to his own age being perfect, Ragnar was one of three kittens we adopted when we realized that all the barn cats we had gotten when we moved to our country home were about the same age, and they were all getting up in years. Siggi and Svarti had been in the care of the Roscrea Cat Rescue Ladies since they were extremely tiny (Siggi had been found near the dead body of his mother on the road, so young his eyes were still closed, and was actually bottle-raised), hence loved people.

> The most common illness in cats is Feline Leukemia Virus or FeLV. It is highly contagious, spreading to unborn kittens. The illness spreads through saliva, nasal secretions, urine, feces, and milk. Cat to Cat transfer may also occur via bite wounds and grooming. 2-3% of all cats are affected by this virus. Vaccination is the only way to protect your cat from this fatal disease.

My husband was choosing with an eye towards a big brave male to replace, in the course of time, our current (neutered, but still believes he's a tom) barnyard king, so got the liveliest, most affectionate, and least fearful of the group. Hence, Ragnar was brought into a situation where he had a pair of "brothers" his own age, who were still young enough themselves to see a strange cat as a playmate rather than an enemy, and who also had been raised to believe that people were their friends. Ragnar's group actually arrived from the St. Anne's Hospital cat colony while we were selecting the other two.

When we saw Ragnar for the first time, we realized that he had to be a recent descendant of Hagan, our late Norwegian Forest Cat stud tom - who, with the persistence and ingenuity of toms everywhere, had managed an unofficial mating with a moggy female who then took off for the hills. In fact, my husband's first words on seeing him were, *"My god, that's a Forest Cat!"* Ragnar looked exactly like Hagan's more official children – long black fur with an unusual silver undercoat, long ear-tufts, long toe-tufts, thick mane and furry "breeches", thick fluffy tail, and that triangular Forest Cat face (he grew up to be indistinguishable, except for his smaller size, from Hagan's purebred kittens).

St. Anne's Hospital lay on a direct line between our house and that of the moggy's original owner, and their cat colony was notably inbred – all black, with longhairs showing up regularly (the long-haired gene is a recessive in cats). Since Hagan had only died a few months previously, leaving us heartbroken, the discovery of a descendant of the lost litter – not to mention the chance to repair a little of the harm done when the pregnant female headed out to fend, and continue breeding, for herself – really heartened us.

Ragnar wasn't in the best condition when we got him: we thought at first he would lose the sight of one eye; he sniffled a lot; and he slept so much that his heroic name was quickly shortened to Rug. We got the eye drops to him in time, which he didn't seem to appreciate much, and filled him with antibiotics, which he did, since they came cunningly mingled with a large proportion of wet cat food. Once he realized that we really weren't going to eat him, and recovered from his cat flu and eye infection, Ragnar became a wonderfully affectionate cat, though he has retained the hunting drive and innate caution of his feral days.

As he did when he got to our house, he still lets Siggi and Svarti investigate any new situation while he hangs back to see if something eats them before he goes in (Svarti turned out to be a decent ratter, and Siggi became a positive demon hunter; both became very fine pets, and good company for Ragnar). Very few feral cat stories have as happy an ending as Ragnar's tale, and not all circumstances are as ideal as those under which we acquired and domesticated him. Nevertheless, with goodwill and patience, it is possible for humans to provide at least some wild cats with happier and healthier lives, as pets, working pets, or barn cats.

CHAPTER 3: THE LIFE CYCLE

CONCEPTION AND BIRTH

Most female cats come into season in the spring and give birth in the early summer. But this isn't always the case. Kittens can be born any time of year, and if you discover a litter of "Christmas Kittens," it's important to make sure the mother cat has a warm, safe place to put them, even if it means bringing a heater into an outbuilding. Fortunately mother cats are pretty resourceful and the mama about to give birth will usually find such a warm place on her own if there is one to find. Borrowing a chickens' nest is a popular option, as is an old tool box somewhere up in the rafters of the barn.

If you can, the best option is to bring a mother cat inside the house when she is near her due date (we do this, but not everyone can). Put her in a small room like a closet or bathroom, where she can't get out. Even not housebroken cats will usually use a litter tray when locked in a small room; and an outdoor cat will feel safer in a small space. Outside the house, a quiet shed or outbuilding is a good place. If you can't do this, you may not see the kittens until Momma decides to bring them to you when they are already several weeks old. This is not the end of the world, but kittens who are handled from birth are easier to domesticate, therefore less work in the long run.

Make sure she has plenty of food and water; and a choice of boxes to nest in. Being a cat, she may still chose to have her babies in the bathtub or the old watering trough, but you've given her more than one option, so she may just accept the box. Cardboard is fine: the important thing is for it to be smooth, with no tiny holes or slates for a baby to get stuck in. Cover the bottom with an old towel or discarded clothing, and have a towel or cover ready to put over the top of the box after the kittens are born. Kittens' eyes need protection (even though they are closed at birth), Mother Cats know this and will always look for a dark place to have their babies.

A towel set ¾ of the way across a box is perfect for them. About 24 hours before she is ready to give birth, a mother cat may get restless, repeatedly try to get outside and may even "call" as if she is seeking a mate. A few mother cats even go into "heat" just as they are giving birth (and can get pregnant). This is another good reason for locking Mommy up if you can. Even if you want more kittens it's not healthy for a nursing mother to be carrying a second litter (ideally breeding queens' litters are spaced 1-2 years apart, but this requires being able to contain Mommy as soon as she starts thinking about going into heat).

An outdoor cat will look for her nest at this stage, searching about the barns and hay shed for a safe, tom cat and dog free zone. Most cats give birth with no trouble at all; usually in the middle of the night. Indoor cats often give birth on their owner's beds, since that is where they feel most safe. Savvy barn cats know they need to hide, which is why a locked up barn cat will probably go ahead and use the box you've provided.

If she hasn't figured out how to crawl out of the third story window already (cats can get out of a space no wider than their head). After her restless period (during which she may stop eating or drinking) she will settle down and start licking her vagina area over and over again. This cleans the birthing area and helps bring the labor along. If she has not already started purring – usually a deep "growling" rhythmic purr, she will probably start now. Best guess is that this is a sort of self-relaxation technique. Be aware that it does not necessarily mean that all is completely well with the cat: cats also purr at times when in severe pain.

However, it is normal, and definitely not a dangerous sign as crying out in pain is. As soon as the kitten's head appears, the licking will increase and most of the time the kitten drops out quickly. The mother cat must remove the sack around the baby before it can breathe, then rolls it over to lick the umbilical cord, which is still probably running into her unless the placenta just squirted out right after the kitten (uncommon). NEVER pick up a kitten at this stage (unless it's a life or death emergency).

The kitten is still attached to the afterbirth which is inside the mother and the kitten, the mother, or both can bleed to death if it's pulled out too quickly. Let her deliver the afterbirth naturally. She will probably eat it. This may look odd to you if you haven't seen it before, but it is very good for her. You do not have to worry about tying and clipping the umbilical cord; Mommy Cat knows what to do. ONLY intervene at this stage if kitten is stuck, as described in the next paragraph. Otherwise, just let mother alone to get on with things.

Soon the kitten (perhaps still attached) will squirm its way over to find a teat and start suckling. If you notice a baby cast off to the side, it's all right to gently (do not pull) move it towards the mother. Keep an eye on it, mother cats often know if there is something wrong with a kitten, even at birth. The kitten may just be weak from the birth process and recover quickly. It could have a medical problem and be rejected by the mother cat. Some mother cats will eat kittens that died in the birthing process, or even several days after birth, which is also natural.

"The worth of a kitten from the time it is kittened until it shall open its eyes is a legal penny; and from that time until it shall kill mice, two legal pence; and after it shall kill mice, four legal pence; and so it shall always remain...

The qualities of a cat are to see, to hear, to kill mice, to have her claws entire, to rear and not devour her kittens, and if she be bought and be deficient in any of these qualities, let one third of her worth be returned" (Venadotian Code, 10th century Wales).

At this time:
1 penny = a lamb, kid, goose, or hen
2 pence = a cock or gander
4 pence = a sheep or goat
(van Vechten, pp. 161-62)

Very few, as the Welsh Venadotian code indicates, seem to get their wires crossed between "eating placenta" and "eating live, probably healthy, kitten" – not a species-survival trait! The kittens must be physically protected from this cat. If you catch a cat doing this once, do not breed her again. Even if she is an expensive purebred show queen, this is not a trait you want her passing down to future generations (assuming that you can keep her from eating the first future generation in the first place, that is).

A cat in labor is very vulnerable and nature has made her very tough and resilient. Normally she does not cry out (except for a sharp "MEW") when the kitten is expelled. If a laboring mother is crying, she is in terrible pain and needs help. It's against every instinct she has to do so, because it is a signal to any predator in the area that she and her helpless kittens are in trouble. She will do so if a kitten gets stuck in the birth canal. This is most likely to happen with a first litter or when the mother cat is very small in size and Old Tom is a big fellow. This is another reason for isolating your expectant mother cat if you can.

If you are there (or even if she is just safe) you can help or give her time to deal with the situation. If a kitten gets stuck and she's on her own, you will probably lose both her and the kitten, since she will die of infection if it's not expelled. To help a mother cat with a stuck kitten, let her try and deal with it herself for at least 15 or 20 minutes. She will push very hard, pant and cry out, but most of the time will manage to free the kitten on her own. If things go on for more than half an hour (or it looks like the mother cat is weakening), you can wash your hands (use gloves if you have them) and gently push two fingers down on the birthing area.

If the kitten's head has appeared, it's vital to get the cowl or birth membrane off the kitten's face, so pull this off first. The kitten now has a chance of survival, but remember the mother's life is most important here. She's your working cat, the kitten is a potential worker. If the kitten is pulled out too quickly, there's a chance the mother cat can bleed to death, so again, NEVER PULL. Just push down. In a dire emergency, as a last resort, you can try and force your fingers in and gently tug the kitten out. I've watched the vet and my husband both do this (successfully) and it's pretty scary.

If at all possible, have a partner hold the mother cat's head as she will be in terrible pain and may try and hurt you. She doesn't understand that you are trying to help. This is why, whenever possible, you CALL THE VET before things get this far. Vets are trained to pull out the kitten (or do an emergency C section). Sadly, most of the time that a kitten gets stuck, the kitten itself dies during or shortly after the process. Don't give up too soon. Let the mother cat lick the kitten and try to stimulate it. Take it away only after she gives up (or starts eating it).

I know at least one huge tom cat we almost gave up for dead, the first born of our best little mouser by a very large Norwegian Forest Cat tom. This was one birthing where my husband had to reach in and disengage the kitten (I also had momma spayed afterwards). One condition that is a serious danger to your mother cat from as early as the last two to three weeks of pregnancy to possibly as late as the end of the lactation period is what is commonly called "milk fever". The veterinary term is 'eclampsia' or 'post parturient hypocalcaemia'.

As described by Little (The Cat, p. 1213), it occurs when a pregnant or nursing mother cannot draw enough calcium from her bones and diet to grow her kittens' bones or make milk and sustain her own needs at the same time, and is 'most commonly reported in queens that have had previous litters and are currently nursing a large litter'. The mother cat's metabolism will almost always prioritize the kittens' needs, so while her milk remains normal, her body is starved of calcium. Eclampsia is usually fatal if not treated as soon as symptoms show.

A cat with eclampsia will stagger, move stiffly, vomit, pant, twitch, and eventually, as her temperature soars (hyperthermia), will go into convulsions and then die. Treatment is a slow IV infusion of 10% calcium gluconate at 0.5-1.5 ml/kg, repeated as needed. The cat needs heart monitoring, as heart rate may slow dangerously or arrhythmias may occur. After discharge, she will receive supplementation of either calcium gluconate at 250-500 mg/day or calcium carbonate at 100 mg/kg day in divided doses until her kittens are weaned.

Prevent her kittens from nursing for at least 24 hours while she recovers (feed them with an eyedropper or syringe). The good news is that if a cat with eclampsia is treated quickly and survives, she is not likely to suffer any long-term consequences – although it is highly recommended to spay her in order to avoid another episode. A cat who has had eclampsia with a previous litter must be watched like a hawk during the whole of the possible danger period.

Checklist For Expectant Cat Moms

• *Have food ready for mom and fresh water in case it's needed. Kitten food is good for expecting moms as it gives them extra energy.*
• *Prepare a kittening area. You can use a cardboard box as long as the edges are soft and you lay down some clean paper or pee pads.*
• *Dental floss, clean scissors and iodine to cut the cord and clean kittens' navels.*
• *Milk formula in case any kitten can't nurse.*

While giving calcium supplements to a high-risk queen before birthing sounds as though it should be an effective protection against eclampsia, in practice it actually increases the risk. The queen's blood calcium is raised by the supplements, her production of parathyroid hormone, which frees calcium from bone when it is required, is suppressed. Therefore, she may not be able to muster enough calcium for both her milk and herself when she begins to lactate.

However, most of the time, you won't have to anything but make sure mother and babies are safe, warm and dry. Even a first time mother will know what to do. Afterwards you may want to gently remove stained or wet bedding and replace it with a new towel or old shirt. But don't worry too much, if the mother cat resists, leave her alone. Make sure her food and water dish are close by, shut the door and go away.

Let mother get to know her babies, she should have anywhere from one to six of them. Almost all mother cats do an excellent job, so they may do it differently. Some are super mothers who spend every waking moment washing, loving, and purring over their babies. Others are working mothers, who prefer to feed and wash their babies, then go off and hunt. They may leave their kittens for several hours at a time. As long as the babies are safe (and not crying), this is nothing to worry about. In the wild (or the barnyard) these two types of mothers often team up to hunt and raise kittens together.

Week 1: Kitten fits in the palm of your hand

Week 2: Kitten's eyes open

Week 3: kitten's eye color may change

Week 4: kitten will begin to stand

Week 6-7: Socialization may begin. Time to re-home

0 – 6 WEEKS

Kittens now walk around freely, with a strut of independence but within close watch of mom.

This is a good time to let them be socialized with humans and introduced to canned food.

It has been highly recommended you do both canned and dry food with cats as when they get to retirement, they may need to be on a more wet based diet.

All members of the cat family, from great lions to tiny barn kittens, are born with their eyes shut, and are completely dependent on their mothers for the first few weeks of life. A tiny kitten is both blind and deaf, knowing its mother and her teat by sense of smell. Most kittens have a favorite teat that they will return to over and over again.

Newborn kittens feed and sleep next to their mother. She will clean them and take care of them until they start eating solid food. The mother will need her litter tray (if indoors) cleaned more often because she is defecating for all of them. Between one and two weeks of age, kittens' eyes open and they become aware of the world.

By the end of the second week, they may begin to try and walk, though not with much success. They stagger about and fall over, but begin to show interest in each other and their surroundings. Their eyes still need protecting from strong light, so keep the towel over the top of the box if you can.

It used to be the accepted wisdom that tiny kittens should never be touched by people; but like a lot of cat lore, this turns out not to be completely true. While it's not good for infants to be handled a lot (which is why small children must never be left with a new litter unsupervised), it turns out that small amounts of human touch at an early stage helps produce very tame and friendly adult cats.

A good rule of thumb is to pick each kitten up at least once or twice a day for a minute or two. Keep it where the mother can see it (you don't want to upset her), and hold gently in your hand and stroke it lightly.

Kittens will begin to escape, looking for interesting things to explore. They may begin to form alliances with other kittens. You may see kittens engage in play fighting or what looks like hunting behavior. All of this is normal and part of their natural development.

Then put it down back next to its mother and repeat with all its siblings. This is also a good time to sex a kitten, which is easier done in the first days after birth than it will be again for some time. By the second week it gets harder to tell sex as the boys develop, so do it quickly. When it doubt ask the vet when the kittens have their first checkup.

By the time they are eight weeks old it becomes easier to tell again. By then the boys look rather more like boys in the under-the-tail region, though they won't get their full male development until they are about six months old. Third week, and kittens will be wide eyed, cute, and starting to play with each other. At this age they will probably hiss at you when you pick them up.

This is normal. It's like two-year-old human children who have just discovered the word, "No!" Keep picking them up. In fact, now it's time to start picking them up three or four times a day. If the kittens are outside, continue to make sure mother is comfortable with you there or she may move her kittens. Being a cat, she may do this anyway, but if she's happy she's less likely to. You can start playing with kittens this young as long as it is done gently.

They start responding to moving fingers and string, though they can't follow them very far. Kittens begin to show an interest in getting out of the box, though they probably can't quite make it.

FOURTH WEEK — ESCAPEE TIME!

Kittens are now everywhere! They are up and out of the box; climbing, active, play fighting, chasing tails, jumping on small bugs, and purring loudly. The also jump fast and are easily startled. If they live outside, they are starting to follow their mother about, but she will try to insist they stay in their hiding place. The mother cat is still nursing and cleaning them, but they start to show interest in sniffing her food.

Her food is too big for them, but you can put down very shallow dishes of cream of wheat, scrambled eggs or cat milk for them. Don't use untreated (that is lactose-free) cow's milk, it can make them sick. They will begin to nibble at the food, and the more they eat it, the less their mother will wash up after them.

Another good reason to keep mother and babies inside: she will now litter train them (if you put a small pan in with very low sides that kittens can get over). Kittens learn by doing and this is the easiest time to learn. This way, even if the kittens grow up to be outdoor barn cats, you can bring them indoors when you need to (isolating without food/water after midnight before spay/neuter surgery, illness, injury, etc.)

FIVE WEEKS — CHAOS RULES!

Everything from last week, only more so. No box now, kittens are everywhere. If momma has hidden her kittens from you, this is when she is likely to bring them out to show you. If kittens are scared of you, present bowls of food and make a fuss over momma cat. If she loves you, they will soon lose their fear of you (if she's feral, see the part on taming ferals in chapter 1 under "Affection"). This is still a good age to domesticate skitty kittens. They will almost always play with a string: it attracts their hunting instincts. Let older children play with them as much as they like, as long as they understand that kitties this age are still fragile.

Kittens continue their skill building by adding running, pouncing, and leaping to the many things they can now do. They often fall asleep at the drop of a hat, as growing up is hard work, so take care when playing with kittens that you make sure you are not overdoing it. They love to play with a variety of toys, strings, toes and more.

It's all right to gently hold a sleeping kitten, but not to try to keep playing with it when it's tired (small kittens can die from exhaustion and over-stimulation). If you can't stand them in the house anymore, this is a good time to let mother and babies start moving outside. It's still a good idea to locate them in a dog-proof shed or barn; but they are old enough to start learning to climb. Let mother move onto the porch and gradually introduce babies to the barnyard. They will follow her in a line and look very cute.

SIX WEEKS-OUT OF THE BASKET
AND INTO THE BARNYARD

Mini-cat time, they are very cute, and will do everything an adult cat will, only in miniature. They still have a lot to learn, but many mother cats will start weaning at this stage. Between now and eight weeks, mother and kittens should move outside unless weather is very bad. This is the age when the mother cat will begin to bring small mice and birds to her kittens and let them try to kill them.

You probably don't want to watch this (or have the results in your bathroom), but it's an important part of barn cat development. Be prepared, you may also lose a kitten or two to the hazards of farm life. By protecting them when they are tiny, you've given them the best chance at a good start in life.

This is also the time when you want to call the vet about basic vaccinations, as discussed in the previous section. Kittens can feed on dry or wet kitten food and should still be fed at least two or three times a day. Their little bodies use up food quickly, but they will also feed themselves if you just leave bowls of food out where they can get them and the dogs or chickens can't.

It doesn't hurt the mother cat to eat kitten food either: she needs the extra nutrition to recover from nursing. Kittens are also now old enough to be without their mother overnight while she is spayed. It's better to do this a week before everyone goes outside, if you can arrange it.

> ➤ *Avoid having an actively nursing cat spayed if you can: if you can. Vets generally advise against spaying a nursing female, as there is a risk of milk from incised mammary tissue interfering with visualizing the site and contaminating the pelvic cavity, raising the odds of internal infection. The blood flow to the mammaries is also considerably increased during lactation, so a nursing queen has high odds of bleeding more severely than a non-lactating cat. However, if you do have to spay a nursing cat for some reason (e.g., a very early post-birthing heat and probable conception that needs to be terminated for the good of the cat), it is useful to know that being spayed will not impair her milk production. The main hormonal signals controlling lactation come from the brain and the pituitary, and require neither ovaries nor womb – even males with certain types of pituitary adenomas lactate!*

Eight to Twelve Weeks

Learning and growth continue at a fast pace. This is when kittens go from kitten to cat in a big hurry. They will start to form lifelong friendships with other cats and farm animals, particularly horses (cats will often curl up to sleep on a horse's back). Most importantly from your point of view: this is the time when kittens usually learn the skilled hunting techniques they need from their mother and watching the experienced older cats.

At first, they will just pounce on bugs and torture the small animals their mother brings back for them. Soon they will be following her about and helping her hunt. By twelve to sixteen weeks of age, they should start catching their own small game. This is also the age to introduce them to "Giant Killer Chickens": i.e., an old hen who won't hurt them but will scare them to death.

This way you get adult cats who are scared or at least respectful of chickens, as opposed to adult cats who may be tempted to think of them as lunch (my husband is still complaining about the time "my" neutered Forest Cat tom ate "his" prize Silver-laced Wyandotte cockerel.

That bird started out as an ordinary purebred cockerel, and has evolved over the years since its untimely demise into some kind of world-class birdy champion, and gee, guy, it was just the one chicken anyway, okay?). They are now teenagers of the cat world and some mother cats will start pushing them away, in a sort of "Kittens, what kittens? I never had any kittens!" sort of way. This seems cruel to people, but is Nature's way of assuring that the mother cat can concentrate on her next litter.

Other Mother Cats retain lifelong bonds of affection with their offspring, sometimes even nursing them well into adulthood. This is more likely to happen if Mother Cat is spayed and has no further litters, especially if the litter you have was her first. Either way, a Mother Cat will always tolerate her youngsters, even if she hisses at them when they get too close.

As long as the males smell like kittens (forever, if they are neutered at or before roughly six months), she will never push them out of her territory. This is why a spayed mother and her kittens can make the best foundation for a barn cat setup. This is also the best age for re-homing kittens. In the past, kittens were given away as early as six weeks, but unless they are orphans, this is really too young. Eight to twelve weeks is the best time: they are naturally ready to move on and they adapt well to new people and environments.

Four to Six Months

Now young cats are almost grown, mid-teens with all the energy that implies. They still eat a lot, but can start moving to adult cat food (though kitten food is good for them for up to a year if you can afford it). Food put out once or twice a day will do, as long as there is enough of it. Play become serious and males may start to lick their sister's necks and jump each other in mock sexual attacks. Older toms begin to notice them with one eye cocked open, but are usually still tolerant if they believe them to be their own offspring. They should be hunting regularly with growing success.

By three to four months, it's definitely time to check with the vet about a group rate for getting everyone altered, perhaps with a charity discount or 'spay now, pay later' plan. This also gives you a couple of months' working room in case you need to spread the operations out for, say, financial reasons, or because the number of cats you can give post-surgical care to at a time is less than the number of cats you have. Final vaccinations can be given at this time as well.

In Ireland, vets often have arrangements with the local rescue center which provide free altering or discounts on spay/neuter and vaccines for cats adopted from the center. It is worth finding out if any animal shelter or vet near you has such an arrangement, especially if you are about to start a colony or replenish your stock of young cats when your original (spayed/neutered) founders are thinking about retirement. It used to be the standard not to spay/neuter until six months – five at the earliest, in the case of early-blooming queens.

Very small girls, for some reason, often come into their first heat early. However, improvements in technology and techniques mean that now a cat can be safely altered when it is either at least 2 kilos (roughly 4.5 lbs) and/or between two and four months old. Young toms, in particular, often do better with early neutering. If snipped before puberty, Tom will remain a playful and friendly kitten all his life, easily socialized with other cats, and be less prone to prostate problems in his old age.

However, if Tom's neutering was delayed until well into puberty or adulthood, although he may spray slightly less after his operation, he will still spray. So unless he is actually destined to live a luxurious life of total captivity as a stud tom, early neutering is the ideal for the male pet or barn cat.

Kittens will begin to show signs of puberty. Their behavior might change dramatically, as is often the case with human teenagers. Kittens at this stage may try to escape outside as the chance to breed is overriding any issue of safety. If you haven't gotten it done already, it's time to begin spaying and neutering to keep your population under control.

SIX MONTHS TO ONE YEAR

You now no longer have kittens, you have young CATS! Cats who can make more cats if you are not careful (see above) but otherwise should now be energetic, happy members of the barn cat community. Now they will each find their own place in the cat group, picking or joining favorite territories and sorting out their social order.

Most domestic cats will keep growing until they are two years of age. Those with mixtures from the larger Northern breeds such as Maine Coon, Norwegian Forest Cat, Siberian, or recent non-domestic ancestry (Bengals, possibly wild bobcat crosses in the US), may take up to four years to completely mature.

You'll only really notice that when they suddenly increase in size "Whoah, how did that cat get so big all of a sudden?" The large Northern breeds and bobcat (or alleged bobcat) crosses make good barn cats, though "bobcat-cross" kittens need to be watched to ensure they are not so wild that they kill livestock (rare but it does happen). Feeding is now almost the same as for adult cats, once a day with some extra kitten food (or table scraps) to support growth.

Otherwise, the young cats require – like every other cat – plenty of water, fresh air, and a warm hay loft or other den. If they were born in Spring, they may need a little coaxing to get through their first Winter, but if a warm space is provided they soon figure it out. You are now getting late for re-homing, but the young cat will still adjust pretty well to a new barnyard and be ready to hunt right away. Don't give away too near by, or they will just come back "home" to your place (if you give them to someone very close, they may start making a daily multiple food-bowl circuit). They still adjust pretty easily to moving but will need to be locked up for a few days in their new home. Warn the new owner to be sure and do this.

All vaccinations should have been given by 12 weeks. Kittens should have lost all baby teeth by this stage, but may have a few lingering around. You may or may not find teeth around the house, as often cats will swallow their own loose tooth. Sleep is now increasing, confidence is growing, the switch from kitten into cat has begun.

Vacination Schedule

-PANLEUKOPENIA VIRUS [FPV] -FELINE HERPESVIRUS-1 -FELINE CALICIVIRUS [FHV-1/CV]	6 WEEKS EVERY 3-4 WEEKS UNTIL 16 WEEKS
RABIES	8 WEEKS, 12 WEEKS -REPEAT EVERY YEAR-
FELINE LEUKEMIA VIRUS	8-12 WEEKS---1ST DOSE 2-3 WEEKS AFTER 1ST---2ND DOSE 2-3 WEEKS AFTER 2ND---3DOSE
FELINE IMMUNODEFICIENCY VIRUS [FIV]	8 WEEKS---1ST DOSE 2-3 WEEKS AFTER 1ST---2ND DOSE
FELINE INFECTIONS PERLTONLTLS [FIP]	16 WEEKS---1ST DOSE 3-4 WEEKS AFTER 1ST--2ND DOSE
CHLAMYDOPHILA FELIS	9 WEEKS---1ST DOSE 3-4 WEEKS AFTER 1ST---2ND DOSE
BORDETELLA BRONCHISEPTICA	8 WEEKS
FELINE GIARDIA	8 WEEKS---1ST DOSE 2-4 WEEKS AFTER 1ST---2ND DOSE

Kittenhood comes to end and the kitten stops growing. Physical development has stopped, replaced with mental development that begins to form habits. This is the time to establish boundaries and rules for your young, sometimes defiant, cat. Positive reminders and small rewards go a long way.

Your cat is quickly approaching their senior years. It seems like yesterday when they wobbled out of the cat basket and became a fully confident feline. This is when you should be observing them for any rapid changes in health. Senior diet may be suggested by your vet. If you have not introduced wet food to your cat, or have strictly fed dry food, it's a good time to introduce wet food now to help with impending tooth loss.

The cats are young adults: full of energy; few health problems, and most of these are due to accidents rather than illness. Altered animals get an extension of their kittenish freedom since they don't have litters or huge territories to raise or defend. They spend their days and nights hunting, sleeping, playing and following you about.

They are curious, lively, and everywhere. From now on, giving a cat away will uproot it and it will need time to adjust. Until one year of age cats are programed to seek out a new territory, and will take on a new one without much difficulty.

The younger a cat is, the less time it will need to get used to its surroundings and new world. Again, it is crucial to lock the cat up for at least a week before letting it outside, or it's very likely to run away. After a week most cats will accept the smells, food, and new territory, and stick with them.

The old tradition of putting butter on a cat's paws when you brought it to a new home is based on this impulse to head straight back to its original territory. At least in theory, the butter slowed the cat down enough to get it used to the new place and presented it with an incentive to stick around (cats like butter in general). This is not nearly as effective for the purpose as is containing the cat for a week.

FIVE TO TEN YEARS

This is cat middle age. They move more slowly but with more deliberation. This is the age of the great mousers and ratters who have the experience to know exactly how to hunt and the energy to still pull it off. Not as much time is spent in play and exploration (though they will do some of that well into old age); but more time is spent in sleep and socializing.

Great care is taken to groom other cat friends; much attention is directed towards keeping their place in the cat social structure and making sure they get the best table scraps when the bowl is put out. They sleep more than they used to, but still not as much as tiny kittens. In short, they are in the prime of life and good at their jobs.

It's difficult to re-home them at this age, but if you need to, it can be done. Not a good time to move house, but it can be done. Add another week onto the lock up period and if there are other cats about, try introducing the newcomer while in a safe place such as a screen porch or kennel cage placed in the yard. This allows the new cat to smell everyone and lets the old timers smell him and get used to him being there. After a few days you can open the cage and let him decide when to walk out and join them. Use the same procedure if you need to get more cats from a shelter to form a new Barn Cat colony.

TEN TO FIFTEEN YEARS THE GOLDEN AGE

EARLY OLD AGE

Senior cat care involves frequent checks on your cats health. Cats will slow down in their old age just like humans. They may not want to climb or jump around as much as nap.

Hearing loss may occur, as your cat gets older. As long as your cat is in good shape, physically able to get around, and your taking them for regular health checks, they still have a good amount of lives left to give.

The cat is slowing down now, but still able to hunt and get along pretty well. Physical problems may start developing now. Both sexes can develop urinary tract problems, though males are more prone to it. Some males may need retirement and re-homing (or to be brought indoors) because they need special and expensive cat foods.

Cancer begins to diminish the ranks of the able bodied, and old injuries start to case problems. Movement is slower in cold weather; cat joints will ache in the cold just as the joints of older people do.

Most cats can keep working as long as they have a place they can warm up and rest. Just keep an eye on them and take them to the vet if you notice they are in pain. Teeth may have fallen out and some older barn cats need canned food (you can bring them on the porch and feed them separately).

A cat can live without teeth, but only if it has soft food to eat. At some point when teeth are going, joints are creaking, and sleep is frequent, it's time to think about: ***Honorable Retirement***. Some barn cats love what they do, and letting them keep doing it into extreme old age is the kindest thing you can do for them. Even the most dedicated old mouser is going to gradually slow down.

Like any elder, a senior cat deserves certain privileges due to age and station. For some cats, this means bringing them inside your house and letting them dream away hours by the wood stove as they catch mice in their sleep. For others, it's re-homing with a nearby family member who may be getting on in years themselves and needs a friend to cuddle.

Some cats will never be happy living inside a house: they are best moved to patrol a quiet stable, corner of a workshop, or other warm and private place. This is most important in the case of an Old Tom who has lost his status as King of the Territory. In the wild (or traditional colony) he'd just pine away and die, but in a managed colony you can move him (perhaps with another cat he's friendly with) to a quieter spot on the farm.

A garage that needs mousing works great, and if you've litter trained him in kitten-hood, he won't even have to go outside. A blind cat can live for years, as long as they are inside in a place they know and their surroundings are generally left in their original positions. Hearing, smell, and touch are all more significant to cat function than to human function. Cats can also become deaf as they get older, something to take into account when calling or admonishing them.

LAST ILLNESS OR INJURY

Most Barn Cats never reach old age, although more are doing so as colonies become smaller and more care is taking to make sure they are fed and vaccinated. But cats can live as much as 20 years, and fifteen to seventeen is pretty common. As the cat population ages, there is a greater likelihood that elderly cats may experience illness or injuries from which they cannot recover.

Our rule of thumb is: if the cat is not in pain, keep it happy and let it do its job. When life becomes a burden, and the cat is obviously in pain most of the time and will never get better, we take them to the vet for humane euthanasia. The same is true for a younger cat with a severe illness or injury. As in people, the younger the animal, the more likely the chance for a full recovery. A young barn cat may live happily with three legs, but an older one isn't likely to do well unless retired to pet status.

Here is where common sense and a good vet can help you make some very difficult decisions. As discussed before, cost is sometimes sadly a factor, but it will sometimes need to be taken into account. But the responsible farmer knows that it's better to make a difficult decision than allow suffering to continue. That still doesn't make it easy, especially if the animal in question is an old and trusted friend.

"In a report published in 2001, the American Veterinary Medical Association (AVMA) defined this 'good death' as follows: "Euthanasia is the act of inducing humane death in an animal. It is our responsibility as veterinarians and human beings to ensure that if an animal's life is to be taken, it is done with the highest degree of respect, and with an emphasis on making the death as painless and distress-free as possible." Cornell Feline Heath Center - Euthanasia: What to Expect and What Questions to Ask First

GRIEVING YOUR CAT

Not everyone who has barn cats becomes deeply emotionally attached to them; and some cats are easier to become attached to than others. Even if you are not particularly fond of cats by nature, if you take good care of your cat colony, including at least the minimum of daily attention and affection needed to keep them tame enough to catch when they need medical attention, the odds are good that at some point there will be at least one cat who makes its way into your heart. That's just the way things work, this means that the day will probably come when you find yourself grieving your deceased kitty.

Even if the cat was old and died gently, losing them is still painful; and, of course, the barn cat's odds of living to old age even in a well-managed colony are less than those of the indoor pet. Among the questions I see most often, over and over – from people of all religions and backgrounds – are variants on, *"Do cats have souls?"* In my opinion: if you feel the urge to ask that question, you have already answered it.

If your cat was enough of an individual being, loving and receiving love, that you grieve them and care about their afterlife – may even feel, as many have felt at the loss of a beloved animal companion, that you aren't sure you want any part of a Heaven which lacks them – then I can say without hesitation that it is obvious your cat has as much of a soul as any being can have.

On the Christian side, Martin Luther and C.S. Lewis both believed that we will see our pets again. Luther saw it as part of the remaking of a better Heaven and Earth at the end of time (p. 362); Lewis argued that animals actually achieve 'selfhood' and thus passage into Heaven through their interactions with humans (ch. 9).

The vast majority of religions throughout history, as seen via burial customs, certainly did believe that animals have an afterlife and generally end up (in some cultures, were deliberately sent) with their humans. In recent times, one of the images of comforts for bereaved humans has become the **"Rainbow Bridge"**. The author is unknown, but the piece circulates widely, where-ever people mourn their animals.

"Just this side of heaven is a place called Rainbow Bridge.

When an animal dies that has been especially close to someone here, that pet goes to Rainbow Bridge.

There are meadows and hills for all of our special friends so they can run and play together. There is plenty of food, water and sunshine, and our friends are warm and comfortable.

All the animals who had been ill and old are restored to health and vigor; those who were hurt or maimed are made whole and strong again, just as we remember them in our dreams of days and times gone by.

The animals are happy and content, except for one small thing; they each miss someone very special to them, who had to be left behind.

They all run and play together, but the day comes when one suddenly stops and looks into the distance.

His bright eyes are intent; His eager body quivers.

Suddenly he begins to run from the group, flying over the green grass, his legs carrying him faster and faster.

You have been spotted, and when you and your special friend finally meet, you cling together in joyous reunion, never to be parted again.

The happy kisses rain upon your face; your hands again caress the beloved head, and you look once more into the trusting eyes of your pet, so long gone from your life but never absent from your heart. Then you cross Rainbow Bridge together"

PALLIATIVE CARE

The time has come to talk about end of life care. There are many resources which have been provided at the end of this book to a variety of different options for the last years of your pet. Palliative care is one such option. Much like the same care provided to human seniors, palliative care centers focus on treating your pet for pain and discomfort so that they remain pain free during the last stages of their life. Deciding what to do for your cat is a very personal decision and should be discussed with your vet and family.

While the original image of the "Rainbow Bridge" as the crossing to a joyful Otherworld was borrowed from Scandinavian religion, it has now become the image of hope for people of many faiths who have to part from their animal friends. If you have children, you are probably well-aware that losing a beloved animal is often a child's first emotional experience with death. If you weren't already well-aware of that, you will be very quickly as soon as the issue arises. At such a time, it is important for your child or children to know how seriously you are taking their feelings. If they have questions, it is also important to answer them honestly, if as comfortingly as possible.

A funeral appropriate within the context of your faith (or social patterns, as the case may be) may well serve at least one of the same purposes that funerals do for the living around the world: to provide closure and a defined opportunity to show grief. Carrying out some form of ceremony, whether with prayer or simply standing around the grave remembering the deceased, is particularly important for children. It helps put the whole issue of death into context, and experiencing the process of farewell and social/family support through a time of loss may also help prepare them for the day when they must say the last farewell to a human beloved.

If there are dogs, foxes, or similar forms of wild or domestic life roaming freely in the area, be really careful to dig the grave at least three feet deep and pile a cairn of rocks on top. Neither canids[4] nor foxes are noted respecters of graves, especially not the grave of someone they might well have already been wanting to eat. They know what is down there, oh, yes, they do; and kids raise the emotional stakes. After all, the last thing you want in this situation now is for poor little Billy, who just lost his favorite cat, to go outside in the morning and see bits of the dearly departed scattered over the yard).

Cremation services are offered for pets in many places, and may be preferred, especially when a cat has bonded deeply to a family member who might want to keep their ashes (some people have the ashes or fur combings of especially-beloved animal companions compressed into cremation diamonds – but not many, because the process is quite expensive). If you live in a rural area or have to be particularly careful with your finances, a standard pet cremation may not be an option for you. Do not, in that case, try to cremate your cat as a home ceremony!

"Your favorite chair is empty now, where you would lie and sleep. But the memory of our happy times is mine to always keep."

Reducing even small bones to fragments and ash takes very high temperatures; and even if you are able to achieve a fire hot enough for long enough, the visual process of an open cremation is highly distressing to most people. Especially to children. If, for some reason, you must home-cremate the deceased, do it a good way from your house and make sure that children and others who might be distressed are going to stay out of visual range for at least a few hours.

Some children will want to get another cat right away, particularly if the one who died was a special pet (or if you don't have a thriving colony). Other children will be hurt by the idea that their beloved pet could be replaced. Even if you need another cat to keep the rodents down, it is best to wait a bit in this case out of respect for your child's grief.

4-The biological family Canidae is a lineage of carnivorans that includes domestic dogs, wolves, coyotes, foxes, jackals, dingoes, and many other extant and extinct wolf-like mammals. A member of this family is called a canid. - Wikipedia

"The first step to help kids learn how to cope with the loss of a pet is to be honest with them. As difficult as this may feel it's important to tell them the truth! Stay away from half truths and euphemistic descriptions about death. Instead, sensitively explain to your child that his or her pet has died. A child's understanding about death will vary based on his age. According to the Association for Pet Loss and Bereavement, kids between the ages of 7 and 9 tend to have the most questions about death. If your child asks you what happens after death, you can explain your understanding about life after death, but it's also okay to admit that you're not entirely sure.

The second step is to honor your child's feelings. Help your child to express his or her grief. You can encourage your children to make drawings or write stories about their pet. It's also very helpful to have them recall happy memories, which allows them to both grieve and remember happier times with their pet. Kids may need to cry and express their feelings of loss, which is to be expected. They might also struggle with other complex emotions like anger, denial and guilt. Encourage your child to talk with you about his or her feelings.

This will allow you to explain that what they are experiencing is normal and a natural part of the grieving process. Ultimately, parents want to help their children move through their feelings of depression and eventually come to a place of acceptance. One of the ways to encourage your child's healthy acceptance of a pet's death is to find a way to memorialize this passing. Having a burial, memorial or similar type of ceremony helps to reinforce the importance of the pet's life while also marking its death. Managing loss and death is ironically one of the most difficult aspects of life. But if handled correctly, the loss of a family pet can be a valuable opportunity to teach an important, yet tough life lesson about how to deal with loss in an open and healthy way."- Dr. Robi Ludwig "Helping Kids Deal with the Loss of a Pet"

Of all bizarre things, Stephen King's Pet Sematery is worth reading in preparation for this situation. Presented as a horror novel – and it is! – Pet Sematery is also a surprisingly thoughtful and accurate examination of the various strategies by which children and adults deal with death. And, of course, a cautionary tale about the dangers of not being able to accept the necessity of death.

There may not be Wendigos in real life (unless you include people with "wendigo psychosis"), but there are psychological terrors just as dire. I would not particularly want a pre-teenaged child reading this book, since it is one of King's darkest and harshest works. I especially would not want my young child reading it if their cat had just died. As an adult, however, you can (hopefully) learn some things from Pet Sematery which may help you guide your child through their first experience of death.

CHAPTER 4: QUESTIONS AND ANSWERS

"I just got a litter of orphan/foundling kittens: what do I do?"

Almost anyone that lives in a rural area will sooner or later be confronted with orphan or foundling kittens, through natural or ma-made causes. Mother cats do sometimes die in birthing or get run over by cars, and people all too often choose to dump small kittens in the bushes rather than humanely having them euthanized if they can't care for them. What a farmer or small holder chooses to do about this situation depends on many factors.

The largest one being TIME, and how much he or some other family member has to devote to the task. It also depends on the AGE of the kittens. Orphans can begin learning to eat soft food by about their fourth week of life, and are well on their way to self-care by six weeks. This doesn't mean they don't need help, but they don't require 24 hour a day care either. Which newborns through the third week of life pretty much do. If you are faced with a litter of orphaned kittens, you have several choices:

Best option: Find another mother cat and get her to adopt the kittens

2nd best option: If you have time, raise them as orphans yourself

3rd (sometimes sadly necessary) option: give the kittens to a rescue center, preferably non-kill, but one that will at least re-home them if they can, or euthanize them humanely if options are exhausted. Or, in the very worst case, take them to your vet for euthanasia. No one likes to do this; and we ourselves still have a couple of cats from a litter that we got from our vet (he called the Humane Society and they called us) because he could not quite bear to put down lively kittens in perfect health. But sometimes it is either that, or turn them out to a short and miserable life of starvation, fear, cold, disease, and death by car.

The Best Option: The very best thing is to find a mother cat with a small litter and hence spare nipples. She will almost always adopt a new baby or two, if you are careful to get the orphans to smell like her. The best way to do this is a bit nasty for humans, but it works. Rub an old towel all over adoptive mommy cat, then rub a tiny bit of her "cat product" on it (use gloves, of course). The smallest amount is fine. Now rub orphaned kittens with it. Hold orphans to New Mommy and let her sniff them while you hold them.

Be watchful: if she rejects them, take them away quickly. Nine times out of ten, she smells her "cat product" thinks they are hers, wonders for a moment how she made that many, and starts washing the new ones clean. Our best nursing mother adopter was Pishi, a rescue probably-Persian who is not as bright as the average piece of cheese. She was pregnant when we got her; pretty clueless about birthing (my husband literally caught a kitten in mid-air when she jumped out of a box and the kitten fell out of her mid-leap), but she adopted a total of nine nursing foundlings.

Two of them kept nursing on her until they were six or seven months old and even her infinite patience or possibly lack of mental faculties finally wore out. Incidentally, if you have a nursing mother and are willing to either temporarily or permanently foster abandoned nurslings – let your local Humane Society know about it! Of course, this only works if you have a spare mommy cat. It will only work if you (or a good friend) have a Super Mommy cat, who now spayed, will still adopt kittens.

This solves all your kitten problems, except for feeding if the foster mommy is not producing milk. Mommy cat washing them (which they require to stimulate defecation and urination) will keep you from having to do it yourself. An alternative (but sometimes less successful method) to get mother cats to adopt kittens is to rub the new kitten against the body of one of a mother cat's original kittens. It works most of the time and is not as difficult for most humans to deal with. The younger her own kittens are, the more likely a mother cat is to adopt new ones. In a pinch, you can try to introduce tiny kittens to a mother with older kittens (barn cats do it themselves all the time).

But you must watch them carefully for either sudden rejection by the mother during the first week of adoption, or her other kittens accidentally smothering their much smaller step-siblings. This choice still tends to have a higher survival rate than complete hand rearing. The Super-Mommy choice is also perfect for older orphans (the sort that get dumped on your doorstep at about five weeks of age). She will wash, care for and love her new babies. And most important from your point of view: she will teach them to HUNT. You just feed them kitten food from the store and provide a litter tray if they are kept inside.

Super-Mom does all the rest. Not all cats are willing to be super-moms and most take a few days or even weeks to warm to strange kittens. Be patient and don't push. Like people, many mother cats will form bonds with kittens eventually. And some male cats, especially those who are neutered very early, will as well. I call these "Uncle Cats" and they can be very helpful. Be very careful at first and make sure they really are an Uncle Cat, or at least a tom who believes he made these particular babies, before leaving kittens alone with them.

Final warning: Some female cats will KILL strange kittens. It's rare; but the older a kitten is when introduced, the more likely it is to happen. This is why the covering smell is so important to making this work. If a mother cat acts hostile to a new kitten in any way, take it away IMMEDIATELY. You can try once or twice more, but if it doesn't work – GIVE UP and pick another option.

HAND-RAISING ORPHAN KITTENS

When you've got a baby that you are hand raising, you have to be the Mommy Cat. You have to do everything the mother would, and in the early days this has to be done every four hours or so. The sleepless nights only last for about a week, but you do have to do this for at least the first week and not go more than six hours between feedings for the second. The reward can be loving, trusting, utterly wonderful cats. It does take time and work, though it can be shared by different members of the family. Tiny kittens can become ill and die very quickly, this is not a good job for small children. Even older children may not be emotionally able to handle the losses; though they can be very helpful for keeping an orphan warm and feeling loved. This is particularly essential if you only have one kitten to try to raise.

What to feed them: In the United States, UK, and Canada, you can often find kitten formula at your local veterinary supply shop or even feed store. It's not the same thing as the "Cat Milk" sold for older cats, but a special mixture designed for tiny kittens. Often there is no warning, and you are trying to feed kittens in the middle of the night or a long weekend. In parts of Europe (especially Scandinavia), everything shuts down on weekends and holidays. Emergency services for people exist, and for pets in major urban areas; but seldom for rural animals.

We once had a similar problem with a litter of kittens belonging to a milkless mommy here in Ireland. The local vet was not really familiar with orphaned kittens. Most people here in the countryside (at that time; it's changing now) would just have drowned them. In fact, a veterinary receptionist expressed surprise that I didn't do just that! The vet overheard her, apologized and looked up a solution in his animal book. He figured out how much to dilute puppy milk (since many people here raise expensive sheep and hunting dogs, orphan puppies were more likely to be cared for, so puppy formula was available).

The result was a litter of happy kittens, one of whom remained the Ruler of the Barn Cats (he was fixed but didn't know it) until he was fifteen or so, at which point ill health forced him into a cozy indoors retirement. Momma cat had love, but no milk. So we didn't have to completely hand-raise them. The feeding for orphans and kittens of milkless mothers is about the same. Except that once the kitten has been fed, you can hand it back to mother (kind of like the pleasure of being a grandparent – you can give the kid back to the parents).

In a midnight emergency you can feed orphan kittens by mixing canned milk (unsweetened, condensed) half and half with water. Or human baby formula cut half with water. I try to always keep one or the other around, since I never know when I may get a phone call from a friend whose kittens are in trouble. If you have to do this, get puppy or kitten formula as soon as possible. The condensed milk or human infant formula does not have the right ingredients for cats long-term.

But it is better than nothing if that's all you have. Goat's milk appears to be a complete nutrition source for kittens. It is a great deal better suited to their needs and more easily digestible than cow's milk, and may actually help prevent bowel problems. Depending on what's available where you live, it can be fed fresh or mixed up from powder.

The "Hoskins kitten formula" is available pre-made, or you can make it yourself. This consists of:

3 oz (roughly 6 tablespoons, or 90 ml) goat milk
3 oz water
4 oz (8 tbs/120 ml) plain full-fat yogurt. Cow's milk yogurt is fine – the
processing reduces potential lactose reactions – but goat's milk yogurt is
even better if you can get it readily.
3 egg yolks

This keeps for 48 hours in the refrigerator, or 2 hours at normal American room temperature (rather longer at Irish country house room temperature, but 2 hours is the safe timing). When ready to serve, put the serving in a small bowl and put the bowl in a larger bowl of hot water until the food is just a bit above a warm room temperature.

How to feed a kitten between birth and 3 weeks of age:
Pick kitten up very gently and hold it vertically in your hand. Wrap kitten in a soft towel or cloth because it will struggle but make sure the towel is not too tight around its neck. The technique, described in more detail in a later question, is known far and wide as the "purrito wrap". With kitten facing you, place kitten feeder into the side of the kitten's mouth. Most of the time, kitten will begin to suckle, although it may struggle at the same time.

If it doesn't, gently squeeze one drop into kitten's mouth (again from the side if you can). Wait until kitten swallows and starts sucking. If kitten doesn't suck on its own, repeat the process (or if using an eyedropper, continue to drop into the mouth). Kitten will stop suckling - or swallowing if you are using an eyedropper – when it is done. Tiny kittens can't eat very much. Don't worry, that's why you're doing this every four hours, day and night, for the first week of life.

After each kitten is fed, just like a human baby, it must be burped. To do this, move kitten over your hand (or a couple of fingers), in the same position you would lean a human baby over your shoulder. Instead of patting a kitten with your entire hand (as you would a human infant) use the fingers of your other hand to gently tap the back of the kitten until it burps. Most of the time you will hear the burp. If you don't, keep tapping the kitten's back for at least two or three minutes anyway.

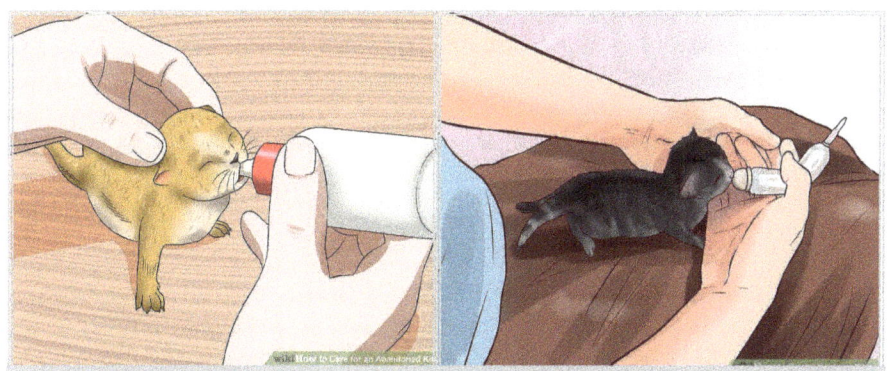

Photos from wikihow: How to Feed a Newborn Kitten Co-authored by Pippa Elliott, MRCVS. Left-Shows bottle feeding with held head, Right-Bottle feeding on lap

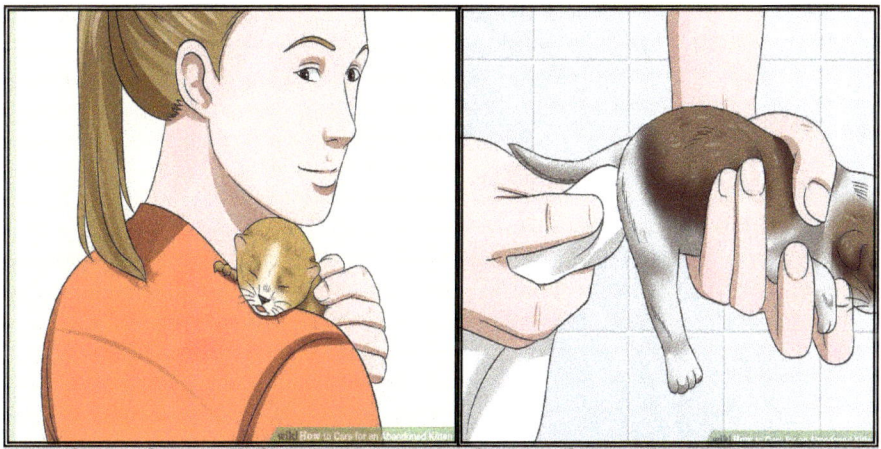

Photos from wikihow: How to Feed a Newborn Kitten Co-authored by Pippa Elliott, MRCVS. Left-Shows the burping position, Right-Shows the proper wiping of kitten to encourage release.

Now for the really icky part, but it must be done or THE KITTENS WILL DIE. You have to help the kitty to defecate. A mother (or foster-mother) does this by licking her baby and cleaning it around its bottom and stomach. If its anus isn't stimulated, a kitten's immature digestive tract will not work and it will form a fatal blockage. To perform this task for the kitten yourself: take a rough washcloth (or rag you don't want later), get it wet, and move it gently around kitten's little bottom in a circle.

If the area becomes red or irritated-looking, put Vaseline on it, just like you would a sick baby. Use only a small amount as kitty may lick it off. Once the baby cat starts washing itself (about three weeks of age), you shouldn't need to help it defecate, or clean it unless it gets diarrhea. If it does, you must help it clean up, as an unclean kitten will also die pretty fast. If you need to bathe the kitten entirely, try to avoid a total bath if you can; a wet washcloth is better.

Clean the kitten quickly and gently with baby shampoo, then wrap it in a warm towel and hold it on your lap until it's warm again. If you can stand it, having a lone kitten sleep (on a healthy adult) as much as possible makes survival more likely. Like human babies, they need body warmth and comfort. You will also have a more well-adjusted adult pet, if it lives. Orphans with siblings will sleep together, but will need a warm hot water bottle (covered by a towel; you want enough heat to last, but not enough to burn your kittens).

Check it often to make sure it's still warm, or use a pet-safe electric pad (ask your vet). Cold can kill kittens even faster than lack of food. Keep kittens in a dark and sheltered place, like a card board box with a towel over it. Their closed and newly opened eyes are light sensitive and can be damaged if exposed too much. Feeding time (and limited handling) are not a problem.

Long term exposure can be. For the first week, just plan on using an alarm clock and get up every four hours to feed the orphans. At two weeks, you can stretch it to six hours and at three weeks they can go all night without a feeding (but feed them three to four times during the day). Most kittens begin to wean themselves about five weeks, but you can start orphans on soft food at four weeks. At four weeks, they are old enough to lick milky food (kitten formula milk with cooked eggs and cream of wheat is a good starter) from the side of a dish. This will make choking less likely, and that's a big killer of orphan kittens.

So if they can eat on their own at all, encourage this as much as possible. Don't do it all at once, continue to offer the kittens the choice of a kitten feeder until they are in their fifth week. By the sixth week even the weakest kitten should be able to lick from the dish and start eating store-bought kitten food. Continue to soak dry food in kitten formula at first.

Make sure their dishes are flat enough to stand in, and that they get shallow dishes of water as soon as they start feeding themselves at all. This is also the age that socialization must begin. If your babies have made it this far (4 weeks) - congratulations, they are probably going to live! Now if you've got a super-momma, this is the time to start letting her see and smell the kittens from a safe distance. Unless she adopts them cheerfully, you still get to be the mother cat, and teach them what they need to know in life. Fortunately, nature has insured that even tiny kittens already possess many of the skills they will need for adult life.

You just have to direct them. Mommy Cat bats her babies on the nose when they bite her, you can tap them on the nose with your finger. You can also tap little paws that have their claws out, and close them up when they go at you. As mentioned above, it's also important to wipe little bottoms with a rough wash cloth after a feeding (Mommy does this with her rough kitty tongue) or the babies can die from complications. You teach them to clean themselves by dropping bits of milk in the appropriate place, when they are about four weeks old.

Finally: it's harder to socialize an older kitten (and six months old is a young cat). It can be done. The easiest way: get another young cat. They will keep each other company and teach each other that it hurts when they bite. Next best idea is to do the same things you do with babies, only more firmly and with more noise.

Never, ever, play rough with kitty. Grab all paws that lash out, allow no biting of people whatsoever (tap the nose, make noise) and hold down for a second (use the "Kitty-Off" button behind the neck if you have to, just don't hold kitty in the air by its scruff without also firmly supporting its rump) with a definite "no." This should be followed by lots of love, petting and attention.

Rewarding of good behavior should help cut down on the problems. There are other tricks for things like ankle grabbing. The large Northern breeds and particularly bobcat crosses are often notorious ankle-grabbers, somewhere in the distant recesses of their ancestral kitty minds, they think that they are at least lynx-sized and you could be prey. Other not so cute kitty ideas, but I won't go into them right now.

All cats have some "quirks" and you have to learn to live with some of them. But rough behavior is potentially a really big problem, especially if you ever have children in your household. Oh, and don't forget that cats are really practicing hunting. So give them toys with strings on them, stuffed mousies, and balls to chase. Let them claw the scratching post and bite the mouse as much as they like. This saves wear and tear on the other members of the household.

"My barn cats are not catching mice. Am I feeding them too much?"

Please, whatever you do, don't stop feeding the kitties, or even cut down on their food unless they are manifestly obese! Go back and read the first section of this book. Not feeding at all just makes for tired, malnourished cats and can cause unpredicted side effects. Like the cats deciding to eat the chickens or scratching up the cabinets trying to find food. Your cats are already hunting: they will do that for fun and do it more often and more effectively if they are happy and healthy.

Unfortunately, some cats just never get the hang of killing their victims (I have a couple of house cats like that), but most will if they see other cats doing it. Females get the idea better than males, since in the wild that's how they have to feed their babies. And in the tame, they still bring back mice to teach their young hunting skills. To quote our cat breeder in Sweden, who would allow her retired show cats the run of the farm, *"it takes a while, sometimes a year, but most of them figure it out, then you may get a 'mouse surprise' several times a day."*

The best solution we've found is also talked about in the first section of the book: get one more cat who's a good hunter. Preferably a spayed female who taught one litter of kittens before she was spayed. Even if your other kitties keep their distance from her socially (cats can be finicky about a new arrival), they will likely watch her hunting and copy her style. Just be sure to keep your new kitty indoors for at least two weeks, so that she knows where home is.

If she's a true "barn cat" and not comfortable in a house, lock her up in an outbuilding with lots of food, water and love. She needs that time to readjust to her new territory. If your other barn cats can smell and hear her, they may accept her more quickly too. Another way to make introductions is to put the new kitty in a kennel cage or rabbit run where she can hear, see, and talk to the other kitties, but they can't really hurt each other. If you have room, just adopt a mama barn cat and her kittens. Be sure to spay and neuter them so they don't increase any further.

But mommy will teach them how to hunt, and while she's at it, she's likely to teach any other cats around as well. We did this, and now almost all our outdoor cats are great hunters. It's all thanks to "Maude the Mighty Huntress", who has taught several generations of kittens and strays what to do. Finally, if you can't do either of these things, you may need to do some detective work. First, look at how many cats you have and the population of rodents.

Since all cats hunt and most are successful part of the time, it may be that you just have too many rodents for the number of cats you have. Like the inside of our house, there may just be too many cat-safe places for rodents to hide (between the floors, the walls, etc.). Many cats eat everything they catch, but most will leave "bits" about for you to step on. Look for these in out of the way places in the yard, as you go about your chores.

Also, try and pay attention to the behavior of individual cats: see who is stalking and looking for game and who is just sleeping by the food bowl most of the time. If you discover that you have too many rodents per number of hunting cats, your choices are: get more cats (not always an option); retire and re-home non-hunting cats (takes observation over a period of weeks, but can be worth it) and replace with a known hunter; and/or seek advice for a good pest control company about animal-safe (include barn cats) methods of pest control that supplement (rather than replace) the cats.

You want to avoid the average feed store poison, since animals who eat the dead rodents can become sick and die themselves. This includes other animals besides cats, including your favorite cattle dog and the pig you were fattening up for bacon. Remember, there is no such thing as total pest elimination. Where there is a food source, rodents will be found. What you can do is keep down their numbers, and that's where the cats come in. In fact, as discussed in the first chapter, it is the original reason the cats showed up in the first place.

"A mama cat has moved in under my barn and had kittens. I can't catch her, what can I do? Am I safe from more kittens for a while?"

First, the bad news: Mommy cat can actually go into heat while giving birth – it's not even uncommon. But if you haven't mentioned hearing the sounds of fighting toms or seen the mother cat rolling about the yard, she's probably not going to do this right away. Toms are one of the greatest dangers to baby kittens, but will sometimes know their own. So a mother cat is better off avoiding heat for at least a month, unless she lives in a cat colony with one protective Patriarch Cat. The good news is that kitties can be spayed, even after they get knocked up. It's not fun, and it can be a bit more expensive.

If you do it soon enough (and five weeks is usually the earliest kittens can spare their mom for two days, plus spaying a nursing female should be avoided due to the higher risk of infection and milk fever), it's not too traumatic. Still, until you find the babies, there's not much you can do about this. Since it seems likely that Mommy Cat may have really have hidden her babies well, you may have to wait for her to bring them to you. You can try making kitten boxes near her hiding spot and putting them in different places.

Cats are notorious for refusing boxes made by their human friends, but will sometimes be fooled into thinking that they found it on their own, if they have a choice of more than one. The kittens will have a better chance of survival if they are in a box that they can't get out of as soon as they are moving about. You have to make sure the boxes are in a safe location (safe from toms, dogs, and other threats), or it may be better to leave them where momma hid them in the first place. On the other hand, if you don't find them until Mommy brings them out to you, all is not lost.

You just have to dedicate a lot more time to "Kitten taming" for a few days. If you're really busy, you can still do a lot by always staying when you put their food down. Even half wild kittens will run to a food bowl. Next step is pet Mommy, a lot. Small kittens will usually climb all over you at this point. If they don't sit by food bowl and play with your own piece of string. Put string on the ground and wiggle it, wiggle it away from you so kitten is not scared by the "Monster" that likes Mommy.

Small kittens will be unable to resist the string for long and will start playing with it, and soon with you. In cases of completely wild litters, when Mommy Cat likes you, but not enough to come near you with babies, more drastic action can be taken. First, get a humane cat trap as soon as kittens are old enough to be running about. Second, catch kittens (mommy will follow). Put kittens (and mommy if possible) in a tiny, closed room, like a bathroom or closed but ventilated outbuilding (a place you will be comfortable too). Get nice, wet cat food and a good book.

Put dish of food at your feet. Be pretty still and read book. Kittens will come over to eat at some point. Next move bowl near your lap, etc. This can be done over a weekend. If the mother cat likes you already, this may only take an afternoon. A tame cat gets over being mad pretty quickly when nice food shows up. Orphan kittens may take 48 hours or so. Obviously you don't have to stay around for the entire 48 hours; spells of reading can be mixed with leaving them alone.

As discussed earlier, this is a great job for older children and adolescents, though probably not while trying to do homework at the same time. Again, the child must be old enough to understand that the kittens much approach them first. Young children should only be allowed in to play with the kittens once they have begun to accept humans as friends, and then only while being supervised. Litter training, an important skill, is done at the same time, just by having the box in the room with you.

This is another reason why the smaller the room is, the better it is, since cats in a small space will naturally head towards a sandy area to use for the nearest bathroom. Orphan kittens may have a few "accidents" but they will get the idea pretty quickly. Even completely not housebroken mother cats usually get the idea. Why litter train a cat who's going to live all its life outside? Two reasons.

First, most cats at some point in their lives have a brief accident or illness where they need indoor care. Being housebroken makes this easier. Second, not all cats, even kittens born on your property work out as barn cats; and it's almost impossible to re-home an animal that is not housebroken as a pet at some future date. Kittens tamed this way are more shy and need to be handled with love and care; but can grow up to be complete pampered house pets and/or really good barn cats.

Don't believe sources that try to tell you that cats "cannot" be tamed unless they are handled before x-number of weeks. They can. Many even become very loving and friendly. They are just usually more skittish than if they have been handled from birth, except for some that absolutely become as tame and affectionate as any bottle-reared kitten. For a wonderful and heartwarming story of how even adult feral cats can be domesticated, see the last chapter written by the famous Yorkshire vet James Herriot in his book Every Living Thing.

The story of Ollie and Ginny and their human friends makes good family reading, and also helps show how much time and attention it can take to fully domesticate ferals, as opposed to just taming them enough that they will live and hunt about your property. The story also points out that it can take lots of time and attention even for a qualified veterinarian of many years standing. A great encourager for children learning to be junior Cat Whisperers, but, warning: have the hankies ready. As in life, not all of the story ends happily (*Every Living Thing* by James Herriot, Michael Joseph, London, ch. 52, pp. 338-344).

"I'm sure my barn cats have eaten baby chicks and rabbits. What can I do?"

Cats are hunters. Unlike dogs, there is just no way to teach them how to substitute one prey for another. A sheep dog can learn to funnel its wolf instinct to kill into herding. A cat is a CAT. It just won't change. Trying to convince the cat not to eat baby birds and rodents will only gain you unhappy cats and an ulcer. That said, there are a couple of things you can do.

First, just realize that you will either have to accept a certain amount of attrition of chicks from your free range poultry (some hens are very good at defending their babies, but no one is perfect), or lock up mothers and babies when they are small. If you have a large enough pond, a mother duck will be able to keep her babies out of danger from cats and foxes, although not necessarily from dogs with a good ability to swim.

Rabbits simply need cat proof – really cat-proof - cages on any farm or holding where cats are kept. We discovered to our horror that our little feline darlings can, and will, eat any parts of a live rabbit that they can pull down through the floor of an unprotected wire cage. Like all non-human hunters, mercy is not a normal cat trait...Therefore you must protect the rodents that you want to keep, leaving the cats to catch the prey that you want them to. For adult chickens, the best safety is prevention.

100

Many farmyard cats are small and do not bother adult chickens as a rule. The larger breeds, which are often popular with small holders, may see chickens (especially sleeping ones) as a midnight snack. If you have an adult cat already doing this, you have to weigh the value of the cat (and its hunting abilities) against the value of the chickens. Or just lock up the chickens or re-home the cat. With kittens, it's a lot easier, just make sure that all babies (and half-grown) cats get to meet the "giant killer chickens" as we call them here.

If a kitten is very small, I do this while it's on a kitten leash, since you don't want the kitten to be truly hurt (and a really mad chicken can kill small kitten if provoked enough). Normally it's enough to just let the kitten get near the experienced chicken who knows all about cats, making noise and flapping her wings in warning. This is enough to terrify the kitten right into my arms. And for the rest of its life, it will treat chickens with respect.

At least adult chickens. This will also have the side effect of helping to protect free range chicks as long as they have mothers with good protective instincts. Alas, this strategy will not work with rabbits. Oh, you can produce unlikely friendships between tiny bunnies and tiny kittens this way. Cats just seem to know that rabbits are rodents who can't really fight back well.

Even if they love their special bunny (who like cats, can be housebroken and even share a litter tray inside your house) they will be happy to eat its brothers, sisters, babies, and parents without thought. So, with the exception of your children's pets who are raised together, it's best to just build strong cages and be done with it.

"How can I feed my barn cats without feeding my dogs, chickens, and other farmyard creatures?"

With dogs, it's pretty easy. Just make sure the food is up too high for the dogs to reach, while the cats can still climb up to it. Make sure there is enough space for all the cats to gather, using more than one food dish if you need to. In fact, a good rule of thumb is to have no more than three to five cats per large food dish. Any more than that, and the smaller, weaker cats are likely to go hungry.

For free-range chickens, it's a lot harder, since most can climb or fly to some degree and can get to most places that you can conveniently feed a cat. The easiest solution is to feed your barn cats when it's dark outside, either before sunrise when you do your early chores. Or just after sundown when the birds have been locked up for the night. If you lock your chickens up at night anyway, you can feed the cats first thing in the morning, before chickens are released.

If you do this, limit the cats' food to what you think they will eat right away, and then feed them again in the evening (just divide up one meal into two). It's a bit more work on your part, but will save a lot of food wastage going into chickens.

Not to mention you will not want your chickens eating some commercial cat foods, especially if you are selling your eggs (or meat) as a small business. It doesn't hurt anything from a small holder's point of view. But while meat-heavy cat and dog foods make for wonderfully yellow yolks, they also may include animal by-products undesirable in even semi-commercial chickens.

"My cats leave me "presents" of small dead animals outside my back door every morning. I appreciate the thought, but, yuck! Is there anything I can do? Should I feed them less so they'll eat their prey themselves?

Feeding less will not solve this problem as even hungry cats will often kill many more rodents than they can eat. Mother cats bring prey back to their kittens on instinct, and may continue this behavior with other adult cats that they see as close friends. This food providing behavior can be transferred over to people. This is because adult cats (especially females) seem confused about humans as a species.

They seem to alternate between seeing us as the all-powerful parental cats (with themselves as kittens) or very large kittens who obviously can't feed themselves and need food brought to them so they can eat and learn to hunt. The mother-kitten bond is the strongest tie in the cat world, so it's not surprising that they carry this over into their relationships with us.

So, obnoxious as it is for the humans, your kitties (or kitty, there's always one) are telling you that they love you and want to feed you. Sometimes they will also provide you with prey if you have been slow to fill the food bowl to their satisfaction, because obviously the colony (which includes you) has a food shortage. Far from punishing you by putting squishy things under your boots, they have decided that there must not be enough food in the house and they need to bring you some more.

An even more disconcerting habit of some cats is to bring live prey - often wounded, bleeding, and panicking in a delightful (to a cat) manner - into your presence and let it loose. Now your kitty is almost certainly trying to show you how to hunt, having determined that you obviously can't know how. Otherwise, how could you ignore all these fun mice to play with? The best solution for both these habits is a combination of prevention and a sense of humor. The prevention comes from learning that funny meow an indoor-outdoor barn cat will make when it has prey in its mouth and not opening the door (and not using a cat flap).

The sense of humor is encouraged by the lines of "dead soldiers" some cats make out of their kills. If none of the other cats (or dogs) take care of them, in a few hours you may want to put on gloves and dispose of the bodies yourself. If the line is very straight or impressive (Maude the Mighty Huntress used to leave lovely tidy rows of dead rats for our inspection under the family car), take a picture to amuse your friends first. And say to yourself, "At least if they're dead, they are not eating my seed stock.". This is generally considered to be more psychologically healthy than repeating "[insert expletive of your choice] CAT!!!"

"How can I control a panicked cat in an emergency situation?"

The first line of control is THE FABLED KITTY OFF BUTTON. That's what our family calls the scruff (loose skin on the back of the neck) where the mother cat picks up the kitten to carry it about. When you do this, be careful not to just grab a pinch of skin or pick the kitten up in the wrong place (you can practice on small kittens by gently picking them up an inch or two when you are not stressed to get a better sense of how it works).

Never, except in a dire emergency, pick up an adult cat this way without supporting its rump as well (keeping 15 pounds of tomcat from ripping you apart during a bath can constitute an emergency). With kittens under eight weeks of age, this is less important, but you still have to be careful to get the neck in the right place. If you have the right place, kitten will cease struggling and pull its little legs up into a ball.

It will still meow and squirm, but it's not going anywhere until you let go. Be warned that the kitty off button is not 100% effective. Some cats are less susceptible to it than others. Any cat that is sufficiently panicked or in pain may not register it. However, I'd say it works at least reasonably well 90% of the time. If you need to hang on to the cat, the best and safest option is what many vets now call the "purrito wrap".

This is simply rolling the cat up in a towel until it resembles a burrito with a little kitty head sticking out at one end and a tail at the other. By doing the purrito wrap, you are painlessly immobilizing all the cat's limbs close to its body, and there is really nothing it can do about it. If the problem is a broken limb, you can still do a purrito wrap, but do not touch the suspected broken limb: leave it sticking out of the toweling (if it's actually broken, that cat is unlikely to be clawing you with it anyway).

An inferior, but quick, option is to get the cat into a heavy cotton or canvas drawstring bag, closing the drawstrings about its neck (being very careful that it can't choke itself – the cat can still thrash inside the bag, so keep a close watch!). This does not restrain the cat nearly as effectively as the full purrito wrap, but it does keep the cat from ripping you up while you take it to the vet or do whatever you need to do with it.

"How do I bathe a cat in an emergency?"

While you may go years without having to bathe a barn cat, occasional emergencies do arise, especially with indoor/outdoor cats. Some minor disasters, like an encounter with a skunk, are probably best dealt with by leaving the cat outside. Other spills (like anti-freeze or lead paint) can be deadly and MUST be dealt with by a vet because they will be fatal if the cat tries to lick them off. Basic rule is: if it's a non-toxic natural substance and has not so smothered the cat that they can't lick it off, leave it alone.

If you find a small kitten covered in layers of mud or an adult cat comes to the door splotched with motor oil, you may need to bathe it. So, for those times you find one of your cats has decided to catch mice among the old asbestos insulation in the attic (this really happened to the owners of an old street-fighting tomcat I knew), here is advice on handling the situation.

First, this has to be a cat you can catch. If the cat is feral or nearly so and has gotten into something deadly, use a humane cat trap and transport to the vet. Otherwise, there's not much you can safely do, since a cat that doesn't trust you to begin with can do real damage to a human being when it's in a state of distress – whether that is from the original situation, or from being forcibly captured. So, let's assume you are only going to bath a cat that is tame enough to come to you for help or petting. First, bathing a tiny kitten is much easier than bathing a full grown cat.

Kittens, due to their lack of life experience, are more likely to dive face first into a large pan of goose grease (really happened at our house. The kitten got washed). Small kittens who are tame will pretty much accept anything you want to do with them as another strange thing that adults want kittens to do. They may not like it much, but they are unlikely to protest beyond meowing and some struggle to get away. It's a good idea to clip their tiny claws first as a precaution (see next question) but it's not absolutely necessary.

The easiest way to bath a kitten as a once-off (as opposed to getting a house pet or show cat used to the idea of regular bathing) is to use THE KITTY OFF BUTTON (described above). Since this is a once-off, rather than a training session, you don't need to worry about helping the kitten enjoy the situation. They are probably terrified anyway, so getting it over with as quickly as possible is a good idea.

You can avoid a lot of trauma by filling a sink with lukewarm water (about the temperature for a human baby bottle) and then gently lowering the kitten in. Keep talking and petting the kitten with your other hand. The kitten may not even realize it's wet for a good while. Gently soap the kitten down with water and baby shampoo (or grease cutting dish washing liquid) everywhere except on the face. Save that for last, because even if kitten is cooperating (and many do), they will not like having their face washed any more than a human baby does, which is usually roughly not at all.

When you have washed off all of the offending substance (you may need a second tub of clean water) then quickly wash the face as well as you can with a cloth. Two people can make this job go very fast and is a lot easier, but one person can do it alone if you need to. For a terrified kitten, use the same process but go as fast as you can, and use a spray rinse nozzle on your sink if you have one. This can scare a cooperative kitten, but isn't going to make a scared one any worse.

Remove kitten from water as soon as it's clean and rinsed, and wrap in a big, warm fluffy towel. Like all infants, kittens can die quickly if they get too chilled. Rub kitten as dry as you can with towel and then release into a warm room. If you wash the kitten in a closed bathroom with a heater, you don't have to worry about it squirming out and getting under the bed. Do not release kitten back outside to mother until it is completely dry. At least two hours for a short hair, four hours for a longer haired kitten.

Bathing adult barn cats is similar to bathing a scared kitten. Except that you now have a very large, strong "kitten" to contend with. Use of the Kitty Off Button is essential and the help of another person is strongly advised. Our 20 pound Norwegian Forest Cat has proved that an unhappy Forest Cat can climb five feet of linoleum tile just as easily as he could climb the sheer rock cliff faces of his ancestral homeland. To avoid having your bathroom wall shredded, get help, if you possibly can. While major sedatives are usually unnecessary and really ought only to be issued by your vet anyway.

If you have the time (stuff on the fur is not contact-toxic and you can keep the cat from licking it for a little while), administering catnip or cannabis (if legal where you live) to mellow this cat out for bathing is possibly not a bad idea. I have seen a happily catnipped cat lying peacefully in the sink as the water rose around him nearly to his chin; if he had needed a full bath, I probably could have managed it alone without any trouble at that point. Having determined that cat must be bathed (and clipped their claws if you have time), have one person hold cat firmly by the Kitty Off Button and support its rump.

Quickly lower cat into warm water in either sink or bathtub (as for kitten) and wash as quickly as possible. Use of a detachable shower head or sink sprayer makes this go much faster and is highly recommended. The off button will not hold an adult cat as well as it holds a kitten, which is another reason for needing two sets of hands. A frightened cat will want to hide, so you may be able to direct the cat's head under your arm as you wash its body. Be sure to soak long haired cats thoroughly with water and clean a mess down to the skin.

This takes longer, but is less painful than having to bath the cat a second time. Once cat is completely clean elsewhere, redouble hold on the off button to wash off the face. Remember: unlike most small kittens, any cat over six weeks old is LIKELY TO BITE if distressed. So it's not just claws you need to beware of, but teeth too.

It's always better to leave a cat bath unfinished than injure yourself. If a cat is just causing so much trouble that you can't wash it at all (and it's 3am or 100 miles from the vet) try placing the cat in a cotton drawstring bag as a last resort. It's a good idea to have one of these made up and kept around for emergencies as part of your emergency animal doctoring kit anyway. I used to use an old fashioned "cash bag" left over from a business I worked at. Stuff cat in bag and gently tighten drawstring.

This is tricky: it must be tight enough to keep the cat's paws in, but loose enough not to strangle the cat. Now quickly soap cat and bag together, and rinse cat and bag together. I've never resorted to this method for actually bathing a cat myself, so I can't say how well it works. I'd advise only using it if you have no other choice. If you can, dry cat with towel, but if an adult cat fights too much, just drop it down and let it run under the bathtub. Don't let the cat out for several hours after a bath. If cat is only semi-tame, make sure it eats first.

Then check to make sure that it's clean, dry, and ready to go. Cat will ignore you for a few days, but is unlikely to run away after accepting food. Finally, if all this sounds like too much, most vets are used to doing emergency cat baths. In an emergency, it may be worth spending the money, especially if you are dealing with a full grown cat. Most outdoor cats can live happy lives without ever having a bath at all, unless they get into something that will hurt them or is so sticky they can't possibly get it off.

Sick cats may need help with personal hygiene (a clear sign of illness is a disheveled cat), but washing the entire cat is not necessary. When nursing a sick cat, wash the affected area only and use cat brush to smooth ruffled fur. Longhairs may also need to have the fur around the anal region clipped if they cannot wash themselves or if they have significant bowel problems. The cat will start washing again as soon as it recovers its health. In fact, that is an excellent sign that your cat is making a significant recovery.

"How do I clip a cat's claws?"

As with bathing, the secret to easier claw clipping is "the kitty off button" This time, really try to do this with two people. One person holds the off button and supports the cat. The other person takes the first paw and opens it up. Press the top and the pad of the first toe gently with the balls of thumb and forefinger. The claw will pop out all the way, and remain out while you hold the toe. You will see that the end and outer edges of the claw are translucent white, but the core is pink. This is exactly like your fingernails. The pink part is the quick, and if you accidentally cut it. It will hurt and bleed.

The white part is dead matter and can be removed without pain or risk. Carefully take either claw clippers (you can buy them at Walmart in the US) or toenail clippers, and quickly clip off just the very tip of the claw, being careful not to nick the pink part. The tip is the sharp part, and that's all you need.

Do this with each digit on the front paws. On indoor cats, you can do this on the back paws as well, but they are less important. For outdoor cats, only clip the front paws. Back claws provide some defense for the cat if it's attacked and allow it to get out of a tree if it climbs one. Some cats are relatively co-operative about this process. Some aren't. If necessary, immobilize the cat in a purrito wrap or a drawstring bag, getting one paw out at a time.

How to Wash Your Hands

This lowly and often-unappreciated skill is your best weapon against the risk of contracting a disease from one of your animals (and/or spreading it to other animals and household members). Among the many things my husband learned in medical school is that no, almost no one really does know how to wash their hands properly.

1) Wet both hands thoroughly and apply a good quantity of soap. Add soap whenever you seem to be running low on suds.

2) Rub the palm surfaces of hands and fingers together, interlocking fingers to scrub between them. Soap to 2" past the wrist.

3) Scrub the palm side of each hand over the back side of the other, again interlocking fingers each time to get the spaces between them. Soap to 2" past the wrist and rotate your grasp to make sure the arm area is fully covered.

4) Scrub the tips of the nails of each hand in a circular motion, one way and then the other, on the palm of the other hand.

5) Do the same with the full nails of the fingers on each hand (to get the cuticle area - you may need to employ a sponge if you actually work with your hands).

6) Grasp each thumb securely inside the other fist and rotate both ways vigorously, several times.

7) Rinse and pat off with clean towel.

The process sounds elaborate, but is quick and becomes second nature after a few repetitions. Wash your hands before touching a wounded or ill animal; again right before and immediately after an "invasive" procedure such as lancing a boil (if the skin is broken, the procedure is invasive to some degree, and the chances of transmitting infection both ways are vastly increased); and always after touching a wounded or ill animal, its feces, or its bedding.

"How do I care for a gravely ill cat who wants to hide?"

At some point, most barn cat owners will have to deal with a cat that is very ill or injured and must be kept inside. The cat's instinct tells it to hide away where no predator can find it. This means going into the smallest, darkest, best-hidden space it can find. It's vital that the cat not be allowed to do this. The biggest danger if your cat is already doing the "hide until I die or get well" number is that he may hide well enough that you can't find him, and then take a turn for the worse.

Some initially minor illnesses such as respiratory infections can go very quickly from "nothing to worry about" to "very bad". Even a vet can find it hard to tell for sure. You really do need to keep a sick cat where you can see them, and not under the bed where they want to go. To prevent the cat hiding away to die, put kitty in a small, warm room, like a bathroom - one he cannot run out of in order to hide from you if he gets worse. You can give him a cardboard box with hot water bottle, if he feels like "hiding."

"How can I tell if a cat is seriously ill enough to need a vet?"

Some problems, like being hit by a car, are obviously veterinary emergencies and need to be treated right away. The same is true for a cat who is unable to breathe, yeowling in pain, or holding its rear and unable to urinate (a urinal blockage can kill a male cat in a number of hours). How can you tell if you really need an emergency clinic at 3 AM? Barn cats often show up at the door with runny eyes, red noses, and coughing. How can you tell if this is an epidemic of severe cat flu, or just a kitty cold going around?

The best suggestion is to take the cat's temperature, if you can manage it. The normal body temperature for a cat ranges from ca. 100 F to 102.5 F; a cat with a temperature of 103 F is considered "fevered". It is very difficult to tell whether a cat is fevered by touch alone, since their normal temperature is so much warmer than ours; I've had cats I thought were only mildly sick, who turned out to have fevers of 106 and were near death. Cats' temperatures are taken rectally and a cat-designated thermometer is another good tool to have in the barn cat emergency vet kit.

It's also a way to check to see if cat has developed a systemic infection after suffering injuries from a fight or other injury. Unless you're a veterinary professional, taking a cat's temperature is best done as a two-person job: one to hold the kitty off button and the other to lubricate and insert the thermometer as you would with a human infant.

Hold as long as you can, up to one minute. Anything over 103 is serious vet time; 106 is near death and needs attention in the next hour or less. Another sign that something is very wrong with your cat: the paw pads and particularly the gums and/or tongue are very pale. This is seen when a cat has lost a large amount of blood (or is suffering from something like feline infectious anemia, treatable by antibiotics but otherwise fatal – and contagious), and when a cat is in shock, whether septic, traumatic, or hemorrhagic.

A cat with pale gums and tongue is a cat which needs to go to the vet immediately. Another way to check the general status is to test for dehydration. A dehydrated cat probably needs to go to the vet for IV fluid replacement, regardless of what else may be wrong. Cats evolved in the desert. This means that, compared to dogs, they dehydrate less easily, as their systems are designed to conserve water and survive areas or times of low water availability. It also means they have less fluid reserves than a dog does and are less inclined to drink enough water for oral replacement to be as effective, so a cat who is losing liquid fast via vomiting and diarrhea is in more time-crucial danger than a dog of the same size.

There is a simple test for dehydration which works on both humans and other mammals: the skin-fold test. It can be done by anyone, no medical training required. For a human, you gently pinch up the loose skin on the back of the hand into a ridge, hold it a few seconds, and let go. If the ridge remains standing instead of disappearing in less than one seconds, that patient is dehydrated. The test is the same for a cat (or dog), except that instead of the back of the hand, you pinch up a fold of the loose skin at the back of the neck/between the shoulder blades.

If the ridge does not disappear within one second, and/or if the fur remains raised rather than smoothing down, the animal is dehydrated. A dry mouth, sunken eyes, and lack of appetite are also symptoms of dehydration, in cats as well as humans. In the absence of the opportunity to get the cat to the vet, you can attempt oral re-hydration.

If a dehydrated cat will not drink, you may need to use an eye-dropper or syringe. Pedialyte, a children's oral re-hydration salt mixture sold in packets, can also be given to cats. A home oral re-hydration solution for cats (also appropriate for dehydrated humans) is:

- *Boil 1 litre (slightly more than 1 quart) of water.*
- *Add to this: 1 teaspoon salt, 3 tablespoons sugar or honey, ½ teaspoon baking soda*
- *Juice from ½ lemon (if you use an orange, reduce sugar to two tablespoons*
- *Mix thoroughly. Give to the cat in small, frequent doses, a teaspoon (5 ml/5 cc) every ten to fifteen minutes or so. Large amounts at one go may cause vomiting, which is totally counterproductive.*

Plain water can be used, but it is much better to give the full re-hydration mixture, as too much water without a bit of salt and potassium in it can cause serious, even sometimes fatal, electrolyte imbalances. Many things like respiratory infections can be anywhere from nothing to worry about to epidemic killers (ready to wipe out most of your barn cats), and it's very hard for the lay person to tell.

If the cat has no temperature and is alert and breathing easily, it can probably wait until Monday to see the regular vet. If you notice at feeding time that you have an outbreak of respiratory symptoms among your barn cats, it's a good idea to take the sickest (or tamest) to the vet. Many of these illnesses can be treated with mass doses of antibiotics and stopped in their tracks, which is a lot cheaper than waiting until they become chronic in your colony. The best test for judging the severity of a respiratory infection is to pick kitty up and listen to his chest.

If you hear small squeaky sounds, gurgling sounds, wheezing, or even sounds of the cat struggling to breathe, it's important to get medical attention soon. In an emergency without a vet, do the kitty version of what you do for a small child with croup. Put sick cats in a small room or closed outbuilding and get a humidifier if you have one. If not, run very hot water in the bath, or bring in buckets of hot water to steam up the room. Do not add camphor crystals, essential oils, or other volatiles that you might add for steaming a human with similar problems.

If a cat stops breathing, hold upside down to drain mucus, slap on back and try to call vet if possible - just the same way you would treat an infant lamb or calf that needed its lungs cleared. Call the vet if you can. Vets have injections that a householder doesn't have and cats are pretty tough. But they can't live without air. If the worst happens, remove dead cat from the others as quickly as possible. Whatever you do, make sure the sick outdoor cats are kept apart from any indoor pets you may have.

If you must bring them into the house, create a separate "sick-room" for the barn cat or cats. Then don't let your pets in it for at least a month or more (or whatever amount of time your vet suggests). The other really important thing to watch (and another reason for locking up the cat) is the cat's food and water intake and output. If kitty stops eating and drinking and drinking is even more important here, it could be feline distemper. Cats can be saved in the first 24 to 48 hours of an attack, but after that it's pretty hopeless. Most cats are vaccinated, but if yours hasn't been, this is a major danger.

If he isn't, get him his shots as soon as the vet will give them, and shots to all the rest of your cats as well. A number of conditions can cause a cat to stop urinating or defecating. The vast majority of them are either medical or surgical emergencies. Many vet clinics will do a limited amount of "special needs" work either themselves or by referring you to someone who can, if payment is an issue. Then, when you are employed again, you can remember the vet or organization that helped you out with a donation to help out someone else. It's to everyone's benefit to keep pets (and people) healthy. An outbreak of something like distemper must be dealt with at once, as some of these dangerous diseases can spread like wildfire. Thankfully there are vaccinations to prevent most of them, and it's worth having your barn cats protected if you possibly can.

"How do I get my cat to take a pill?"

This can be one of the more difficult tasks a cat owner has to face, and it doesn't matter if Tiddles is a pampered house-pet, a street-fighting tom, or the Great Lord of the Barnyard. Almost all cats hate to take pills. It's amazing how quickly a five-pound ball of fluff can turn into a man-eating saber toothed tiger when faced with one. Fortunately, there are a few things you can do to ensure that the pills go into the cat, without the cat's claws (or teeth) going into you. But first the bad news.

Despite what a rural, large animal vet may tell you, cats are not dogs (or sheep, or cows, or chickens, etc). They WILL NOT take pills that are either disguised by or ground up into food. This is because cats have very highly developed senses of taste and smell. They will notice the difference every time and either spit out the pill or ignore the food. 99 percent of cats will do this.

If you are very lucky (or your cat is very old), you may get away with mixing some medicines into wet cat food. So it is worth trying, but almost always fails. For nursing kittens, you can mix the required amount of medicine into a syringe and feed it to them with kitten formula. It is only advisable to do this under the direction of a vet, since tiny kittens require very small amounts of medication at a time. Okay, so you've tried to hide the pill in the food and kitty has laughed at you (and the dog has eaten kitty's medicated treats). Now it's serious pill time. While no cat likes to take a pill, cats vary dramatically in how much they will resist it. The first time you give a pill, you can try:

1 – Put Kitty on table, bed, or other level surface

2- While petting cat, gently grasp the Kitty Off Button on the back of the neck and very gently pull head back at an angle with the cat's mouth in a position you can reach.

3 – Place pill in BACK of the cat's mouth, near the throat. DO NOT PUSH the pill down the throat, this can kill the cat. But leave it as far back as you can without pushing. Now, hold the cat's mouth shut (as with most hands-on cat chores, this is easier with two people).

4 – Stroke the cat's throat until you see the cat swallow the pill. If you have a second person to help, they can keep holding the Kitty Off Button until pill is swallowed.

5 – Open cat's mouth and make sure pill is really gone. If it isn't, or cat has spit out the pill (happens even to experienced cat pillers), repeat the process.

My husband uses a variant technique which involves sneaking up behind the cat; grasping the Kitty Off Button and pulling the head slightly back with one hand; and popping the pill in with the other before using that hand to keep the cat's mouth closed until it swallows. He can do this before the cat knows what's happening. He also grew up with a Korat who required a pill every day and never stopped fighting the process like a maniac for her remaining fifteen years of life.

If cat struggles a great deal, purrito-wrap it or put it in a drawstring bag, as described above. Also, you can ask your vet or pet store if they have a "cat pilling" device. This is a plastic tube that lets you put the pill in the end and is shaped to go into the cat's mouth at the proper angle. It also has the advantage of keeping your hands away from Kitty's teeth.

Remember, your cat doesn't really hate you, it just doesn't understand why you are doing something to it that it finds either painful, unnecessary or both. Millions of years of evolution tell it to try and get away, which may mean biting or clawing you to the bone. Your job is to get things over with as quickly as possible, with as little harm to either the cat or yourself as can be managed.

"What if I have a lot of cats to pill at the same time?"

As barn cat owners, we have several times confronted the need to pill a number of cats at once. All you need is a serious outbreak of a contagious (but treatable) disease like cat flu or worms to have weeks' worth of pill giving. Again, just mixing ground pills with food won't work (although it's better than nothing if you've cats you can't catch. In that case, try a very smelly food like oily fish to mix it with and cross your fingers). What we do is make a list of all the cats (by name) and then bring each one into the porch or kitchen as we catch it.

We pill it and mark it as pilled on the list. Then we start the process over the next day (or time of day). With Barn Cats, we ask the vet for once a day dosages whenever possible. The cats wise up to things pretty quickly, and you may not get everyone as often as you'd like to. We give each cat a special treat (like raw beef or fish) before we put them back out.

That way they associate coming inside with good food as well as the hated pills. If you have to, you can cut down on their outside food during the week medicine is prescribed. In that case, be sure each cat gets enough food before it goes back outside again to last the entire day. Hungry the next day, they will be more likely to allow themselves to be caught. Fortunately, the need for mass cat pilling is unusual in a healthy barn cat colony.

"Can I castrate my male kittens by banding? It works so well (and cheaply) on larger livestock."

A lot of farmers have looked at a litter of kittens and wondered, *"Couldn't I just band the boys the way I do male lambs and save the trips to the vet?"* Sadly, no. You can't. Kitty testicles do not dangle down the way lamb testicles do; they are snugged right up against the body (and may, or may not, have descended at birth, though they are almost always out by six to eight weeks. But even if they're present, they're very tiny and not at all easy to even find, let alone mechanically isolate).

So you can't neuter a tom (or a dog, for that matter; same testicle-architecture issue) by banding. There really is not a safe and humane way to home-neuter a male cat. If there were, the over breeding problem would be considerably less than it is. If you live way out in the country, you may well still know one or two of those crusty old farmers who castrate larger livestock the very old-fashioned way – with their teeth.

This, I am reliably informed by someone who has been doing it for a very long time, involves taking a good grip on the relevant organs, locating the vas deferens[5] (he called it, "that tube, you know yourself, where the stuff comes through", but I got the idea) and major blood vessels, and biting down on them (above the testicle) until a double crunch is heard and felt.

Never having actually seen the process in action, I can't comment on how humane it might or might not be compared to other methods of castrating livestock. But regardless, cat anatomy suggests that you probably can't do this with a cat, and humane concerns suggest that you probably shouldn't experiment with doing it either.

"Can I catch any diseases from my cats?"

Most diseases from which cats suffer are not transmittable to humans. However, a few of the exceptions have the potential to be serious threats, and if you are in an endemic area, you need to be aware of them. From the common and relatively minor, to the fortunately rare but often-fatal, the main diseases that you can catch from a cat are:

---

5 The ductus deferens, also known as the vas deferens, is a tiny muscular tube in the male reproductive system that carries sperm from the epididymis to the ejaculatory duct.-
https://www.innerbody.com/image_repmov/repo26-new2.html

Cat Scratch Disease/Fever – Bartonella hensellae:
This is usually contracted just as described on the tin; from a bite; or via cat fleas. The symptoms are swelling and redness at the site, and the local lymph nodes may become inflamed and tender. Some people also get "flu-like" systemic symptoms – fever, sore muscles, headache, and fatigue. Without antibiotics, it can take several months to clear; antibiotic treatment is generally only given in more severe cases.

While presenting little danger to the healthy person, cat scratch fever can be dangerous to the immuno-compromised, old, and very young, as the bacteria may be able to survive in the bloodstream and colonize various vital organs if not met with a healthy immune response. *"Pasturella multocida"* is a bacterium very commonly found in the mouths of cats and dogs, transmitted by bites.

Any animal bite should be thoroughly washed and cleaned out; if major signs of inflammation (pain, swelling, redness, heat) are seen within 48 hours, a course of antibiotics is required: severe local infection and systemic infection are both possible.

Lyme disease (Borrelia bergdorferi): While you cannot catch Lyme disease directly from a cat (or another human, or a white-tailed deer), cats can most certainly act as reservoirs to pass the disease on to you via shared ticks in the garden or woods.

The best ways to keep this from happening are: prevention (protective anti-tick treatment); observation (check cats for ticks regularly; remove any tick found; watch that cat for the "bullseye" rash forming under its fur, or signs of not being well); and, if necessary, treatment. In both cats and humans, Lyme disease, if diagnosed early, can easily be treated with antibiotics without the long-term systemic consequences for which the disease is infamous. If your cat has it, get that cat to the vet before it shares the bacteria through the local tick population.

Plague (Yersinia pestis): Yes, the plague, the same disease that ravaged medieval Europe. Plague is endemic in the Southwest and West Coast of the US; several people die of it yearly; and somewhere around 20-25% of US cases in humans are tracked back to a domestic cat that interacted with the wrong rodent (prairie dogs are notorious plague reservoirs; squirrels are also suspected).

There are issues with plague vaccines; you can't just ask your vet (or local GP, for that matter) for a shot. If you live in a plague-endemic area, flea treatments become a major priority, and it is strongly recommended both to keep a close eye on the health of your cats and dogs, and – if Puss or Rover shows any sign of illness and then you start feeling poorly, get to the doctor at once.

Plague is treatable with antibiotics if it is diagnosed and treatment is begun early enough. Most people who die of it in the US, do so because they wrote the early symptoms off as flu and then were incapacitated too fast to call for help, or else did not get treatment in time to save them. The chances of you actually catching bubonic plague from your cat, even if you live in an endemic area, are probably like a negative version of "winning the Powerball" odds. It's rare, it's very rare indeed. But after "park ranger", "rural-dweller in endemic area with domestic livestock" is the highest-risk category, and cats are markedly vulnerable.

Protozoal diseases – Toxoplasmosis, giardia, cryptosporidium. These are all single-celled parasites which enter the host's system orally and are usually passed on via feces, directly or through spread into the water system. Be sure to wash your hands thoroughly, with soap, after handling cat doings in any way. Toxoplasmosis is not normally a significant danger to a healthy person. The protozoa usually encyst and remain latent for life.

It is a significant danger in several cases of vulnerability: pregnancy and infancy (the disease can also be passed mother-to-fetus), immuno-compromise of any sort, and old age (as the immune system gradually weakens). People in these categories should particularly avoid contact with animal feces of any sort. Giardia is a scourge of outdoor water sources almost everywhere.

It is characterized by particularly messy, smelly, persistent diarrhea. Giardia is easily treated, in both humans and cats, with a course of the antibiotic metronidazole[6]. Cryptosporidium is usually spread through contaminated water, though like all pathogens with a characteristically oral-fecal spread, it may also be transmitted directly through poor hygiene or unhygienic food preparation.

The symptoms are chiefly repeated bouts of watery diarrhea; there may also be respiratory involvement, and it can be transmitted by coughing. Treatment is primarily symptomatic (controlling the diarrhea) and supportive (making sure that the cat does not dehydrate, and does get adequate nutrition; it may lose its appetite). If bloody or extremely copious diarrhea occur, or the cat is showing other signs of severe unwellness and/or running a fever, that cat needs urgent medical care: it may have a secondary bowel infection, and it may be at risk of death by dehydration.

All of these things are equally true of humans. The prescription drug nitazoxanide is used for treating cryptosporidiosis[7] both in humans and in cats (cat dose: 25 mg/kg, or ca. 12 mg/lb). Be aware that in cats it causes vomiting and foul-smelling diarrhea; but a few days of nasty isolation room cleaning for one cat is probably preferable to an ongoing concern about family outbreaks.

To minimize the risks of transmission, an animal who is suspected to have either of these conditions should, ideally, be isolated in a room that is easily cleaned and disinfected until it has finished the course of metronidazole (giardia) or ceases to have diarrhea (cryptosporidium – although the cat will still be potentially contagious for weeks).

---

6 Metronidazole is used to treat bacterial infections in different areas of the body
7 Cryptosporidiosis is a diarrheal disease caused by microscopic parasites

As giardia and cryptosporidium are both most commonly contracted through contaminated water, and are likely to further contaminate any water into which an infected creature's excrement ultimately drains, they are considered public health problems. This is especially important if you are on a public water system. Alerting your local authorities to diagnosed or suspected cases may save human lives and well-being (probably your vet and/or GP will do the heavy lifting of calling the appropriate official people if a diagnosis of either is confirmed).

Rabies: If you do not live in a rabies-free country, your concern for your own safety and that of every mammal on your property should dictate that you have all your cats vaccinated for rabies if at all possible. As domestic animals go, cats and dogs are the likeliest to contract rabies. If an animal is showing symptoms suggestive of rabies (foam at the mouth, inability to drink, unsteady gait, uncharacteristic aggression), do not attempt to deal with it yourself unless you have no other choice.

Call animal control. If you have no other choice, I hate to say this, but your options are down to shooting the cat from a safe distance, bagging its body without touching it or any fluids present (and make sure any residue is bagged and incinerated), and taking it to the local vet – or trying to capture it in hopes that the problem is not rabies, with full knowledge of the fact that you, personally, are probably looking at an unpleasant series of inoculations if the animal tests positive. Kittens are usually vaccinated for rabies at 12-16 weeks (after their maternal-derived antibodies can no longer interfere with the vaccination). A booster at 12 months and thereafter every 1-3 years is recommended; your vet will be able to explain the optimum course to you.

Ringworm: You can catch this fungal skin infection from your cat, and your cat can catch it from you. The treatment is usually oral for cats, topical for humans. It is not particularly dire, but if it covers a large area or persists for a long time, scratching and general damage may lead to a nasty skin infection.

Salmonella: Hunting cats are likelier than house cats to pick up this bacterium, as it is present in many of their prey items. You can avoid catching it from your cats by wearing gloves when dealing with their feces and washing your hands thoroughly after cat-handling or at least every time before you eat.

Worms: You can get many species of worms from your cat, and indeed vice versa. This is discussed at more length in ch. 4. Fortunately, in both humans and cats, worms are usually very easy to treat and present little or no danger if they are diagnosed and dealt with in a reasonably timely fashion.

"Are cats dangerous to young babies? I've heard they will suck a baby's breath"

No, that is a myth. Cats are not generally dangerous to young babies (as long as you don't let them play in the cat box, and practice good hand hygiene yourself). However, the myth actually probably did come from elements of observed behavior. Cats will lie on top of an ill or chilled human, possibly to warm them as they would a kitten who needed it; and since babies drink milk, cats also will show an interest in sniffing at their mouths.

There likely were many cases of SIDS (and other then-undefined, non-obvious causes of infant death) where a cat was found on or beside the baby, quite possibly trying to revive or warm it, and quite possibly also investigating the interesting scent and taste of the mouth area...leading to the cat being blamed as the cause of the death.

If you had heard as an "everyone knows" that cats can suck a baby's breath, and then saw one in the crib sniffing and licking the baby's face, you'd probably think that it was trying to do just that. Having said that, if the cat weighs as much as the baby or more, it probably shouldn't be allowed to sleep on the baby, at least not without some supervision to make sure that the baby is not in any distress. The baby is unlikely to cause much distress to the cat until around 6-9 months old, when human babies generally start really getting into that whole gripping-for-fun (as opposed to simple reflex) thing.

"One of my cats appears to be mentally compromised. What do I do?"

Cat intelligence comes in a range which is, at least comparatively, as wide and varied as that of humans. A cat may seem extremely stupid in some regards, but still be a competent survivor and an excellent hunter due to good physical intelligence and instincts. Having said that, we have had two cats in twenty years that were officially declared "Too Stupid To Go Outside". One was just real low-wattage, and probably would have been fine as a barn cat.

The other, Eric the Dim, was actually defective. However, the myth actually probably did come from elements of observed behavior. Cats will lie on top of an ill or chilled human, possibly to warm them as they would a kitten who needed it; and since babies drink milk, cats also will show an interest in sniffing at their mouths.

There likely were many cases of SIDS (and other then-undefined, non-obvious causes of infant death) where a cat was found on or beside the baby, quite possibly trying to revive or warm it, and quite possibly also investigating the interesting scent and taste of the mouth area...leading to the cat being blamed as the cause of the death.

If you had heard as an "everyone knows" that cats can suck a baby's breath, and then saw one in the crib sniffing and licking the baby's face, you'd probably think that it was trying to do just that. Having said that, if the cat weighs as much as the baby or more, it probably shouldn't be allowed to sleep on the baby, at least not without some supervision to make sure that the baby is not in any distress. The baby is unlikely to cause much distress to the cat until around 6-9 months old, when human babies generally start really getting into that whole gripping-for-fun (as opposed to simple reflex) thing.

"One of my cats appears to be mentally compromised. What do I do?"

Cat intelligence comes in a range which is, at least comparatively, as wide and varied as that of humans. A cat may seem extremely stupid in some regards, but still be a competent survivor and an excellent hunter due to good physical intelligence and instincts. Having said that, we have had two cats in twenty years that were officially declared "Too Stupid To Go Outside". One was just real low-wattage, and probably would have been fine as a barn cat. The other, Eric the Dim, was actually defective.

He got out once, at the age of seven or eight (having been a house cat all his life), and over the course of a whole twelve hours, forgot that he had ever been a house cat. When we lured him back in, it took him a while to remember who we were and figure out the layout of the house he had lived in for several years (he did a lot of other things suggesting that he had no working memory or significant cognitive faculties too, but that was the most obvious).

However – even Eric the Dim could hunt quite well. If he had been born in a barn cat colony, the humans might never have noticed anything other than a tendency to skittishness, though his long-term survival chances might not have been as good as a young male's of normal intellect, and those aren't brilliant without human colony control. Cats can also suffer temporary or permanent mental and neurological damage from physical trauma, disease, and poison. We have one neutered tom who we suspect of having gotten poisoned by eating the wrong rat a couple of years ago (the outer coat of seed grain is normally treated with poison to deter rodents and insects).

He lost much of his sight, some of his hearing, and a great deal of mental or at least psychological function. He did recover some of his capabilities very slowly, but he can no longer go outdoors, as he becomes lost and disoriented in the front yard. A cat that is too mentally damaged to survive outside either has to be reclassified as an indoor pet or re-homed. If the damage includes, for instance, incontinence or uncontrolled outbursts of aggression, sadly – unless you or someone who can take it is a cat-loving saint – euthanasia may be the only choice.

"Can I tell a cat's sex by its color or markings?"

Not absolutely, but there are some color combinations that lean very predominantly to female. Cats carry their color genes on their X chromosome.

This means that a male cat can be red (ginger/marmalade/orange), brown, black, "blue" (gray), white, or any single color plus white. What he cannot normally be is a mixture of any two out of red/brown/black/"blue". Therefore, the odds are extremely high that a tortoiseshell (red and black or "blue") or calico (red, black or "blue", and white) is a female. However, some cats are chimera: that is, their genes are the genes of two different kittens that merged in the womb. A chimera male can be a tortoiseshell or a calico. These boys may well be fertile. A male cat with Klinefelter's syndrome (XXY) can also be a tortoiseshell or a calico, but he is extremely unlikely to be fertile.

If you have a male tortie or calico, you might want to check with your local veterinary college to see if they're doing any studies on multi-colored male cats, especially if you think your lad is fertile – though a Klinefelter's cat will have a normal sex life, and given the noted fidelity of queens on heat, you might never be able to tell without getting an actual sperm count. Recessive colors are more likely to show up as single colors on males for the same genetic reason. A female who gets a red gene and another color-gene will be multicolored; but a male only has one color choice, so if it is recessive (as red and gray/blue are), that is the color the cat will be, though he may combine it with white.

So, with natural breeding, there will always be more solid red or solid gray/blue males than females, since the latter would require matching recessives (and all her kittens will either be fully red or red mixes, probably depending on gender). In fact, in Ireland, it used to be believed that an all-ginger or ginger tuxedo (white paws and front) cat had to be male. That is not the case. However, if you are in the habit of making bets about the gender of random cats, and the cat is either red or gray (plus/minus a bit of white), the odds on it being male are approximately 3:1.

"Do bobcats or wildcats ever cross with domestic cats? I've heard that the Pixie Bob breed is a bobcat cross."

The European wildcat can cross with domestic cats. This is actually a concern regarding the domestic genome mixing into the Scottish wildcat genome, which is feared to be putting the latter under serious threat. To the best of anyone's knowledge, lynx do not cross with domestic cats, and possibly could not. The question of whether North American bobcats either can (appears to be theoretically possible; at least they share the same number of chromosomes) or do cross with domestic cats is another issue, which the "Pixie Bob" breed brought up. That breed was created from what the creator called "Legend Cats", i.e., cats that showed traits suggestive of possible bobcat ancestry.

However, a genetic study determined that there were no bobcat genetics in any specimen of the Pixie Bob breed. In fact, there has never yet been any genetic testing that proved the existence of bobcat/domestic hybrids. One "hybrid" in Colorado, a cat named Rocky, was DNA-tested in 2014. The results showed that his mother was definitely a bobcat, but were inconclusive regarding his father (Rocky's inconclusive test was sufficient to allow his human family to reclaim him on the grounds that he could not be proven to be 100% bobcat; but he ended up at the local zoo eventually due to his tendency to escape from his home).

Having said that, anecdotal reports of apparent bobcat/domestic crosses are extremely common and consistent throughout North America (as are reports of bobcats killing domestic cats). In fact, they are common enough that there are some general protocols for raising suspected "bobcat crosses", and I have been asked how to do this more than once. It is possible – in fact, it is very highly likely to be the case - that all of these animals, like the "Legend Cats" from which the Pixie Bob was bred, are simply large, brown-ticked domestic tabbies with temperaments on the "wild" end of the wide range of domestic cat personalities. However, they do have some consistent personality traits which often require slightly different handling.

These techniques would also apply to a European wildcat/domestic cross; often apply to the large breeds recently developed from independently-evolving semi-feral populations (Pixie Bobs, Maine Coons, Forest Cats); and most definitely apply to any of the other breeds such as the Bengal in which wild cats have deliberately been bred in with domestics (despite the name, this doesn't apply to the Ocicat. Ocicats are totally domestic in breeding and temperament; they're just fairly large and very spotty).

"Bobcat crosses" and their equivalents can make wonderful pets and working cats, but they have to be handled a bit differently from your average domestic cat. They are highly intelligent. They have to be, since at least half their ancestors are wild cats, living without human assistance. That is true whether they are genuine hybrids or descended from very successful mostly-feral populations (Maine Coon, Forest Cat, Siberian) in situations where bobcat/wildcat-like traits were survival advantages.

Which means that even if they're not genuine bobcat/domestic crosses in genetic terms, they might as well be in practice. Like most of the larger and comparatively recently feral-population-derived cats, "bobcat crosses" take longer to mature and grow up. Most domestic cats reach their full growth and settle down around age two. The larger breeds and "bobcat crosses" take about four years altogether. Don't be surprised if kittens of this type shoot up even bigger at about age three. It's normal, but it can be a surprise.

They get so big, you need to do some very strict training when it comes to items like soft-paw, biting, and hunting behavior. It's obnoxious when any cat attacks your guests' ankles, but it can be dangerous when a larger (and sharper-clawed) cat does the same thing. Your babies are likely to want to do it more often, because they are swift and proud hunters by nature. So give them lots and lots of toys and play with them often. Praise all good behavior with lots of love, pets and chuckling noises.

Be swift and constant when hunting is inappropriate (like clawing your hand) or claws and teeth are used on people. To punish, think like a mother cat. For minor crimes a quick tap on the noise with a sharp "NO" (the sound is the main punishment here, the tap is to startle). For more serious crimes (or when kitty is very overexcited and they will get this way), grab kitty by the Kitty Off Button (works on wild felines as well as domestic ones, though I wouldn't try using it to leopard-wrestle) and hold down on the floor or lap.

Now place your other hand on the cat's neck in the position where the mother cat's teeth would be (again not hurting the cat: the mother cat doesn't really bite, just grazes the kitten). Now put your mouth as close as you can to the back of your hand (neck of the kitten) and do a deep, loud GRRRRRR! sound. This is an imitation of mommy holding kitten down with paws (or teeth) and growling. If possible, now turn kitten over in your arms onto its back into "submit" position. Hold kitten firmly but gently and start petting and praising. Sometimes the cat will run before you can do this, and that's all right too. If cat "sulks" for more than an hour, get out a favorite toy or food dish and temp them back over.

Most young cats recover pretty fast, just as they do from bathing, pilling, and other unhappy cat events. Discourage ANYONE, and I mean husband, friends, and so forth, from "playing rough" with the kitties. Except with toys which they can attack and destroy as much as they like. It may be cute now, but it won't be cute when a 25 or 30 pound grown cat bites down on someone's fingers. For biting, we hold our Forest Cat kitten's mouth close for about 30 seconds saying, "NO BITE. NUZZLE AND LICK.

Lick is good, bite is not". Then release, pet and cuddle. Sometimes it takes days and lots of closed mouths to get it through their fuzzy little brains. Some kittens retain the nickname "No Bite" for the rest of their lives – as in, "Hi! My name is No Bite. Sometimes humans call me, 'Get Down From There!'" Like most children, kittens really do want to please their parents, including their human parents. They are a bit confused because normal biting and nipping would be acceptable to a mother cat. We humans don't have the fur to take even mild amounts of it (except for the soft-paw, no-teeth versions that the babies are already using on your eyes and feet).

On the plus side, their extreme intelligence makes these cats some of the most exciting companions in the world. If you have a farm, introduce them to the "large killer chickens" before they are big enough to kill chickens themselves. The imprint will stay with them, and they will go after rats and wild rabbits instead. They also tend to attach themselves to one or two people as they get older. So if you need to re-home any of them, do it soon, while they can still make the transition to another human friend. Linda Graves of Brown Brook Farm writes about her own experience with a "Legend Cat"/possible hybrid. Her description vividly demonstrates that it is ultimately irrelevant whether these cats owe their origin to any species but *F. domesticus*. If it acts like a wild feline, especially if it's larger than most domestics, it might as well be one.

CHAPTER 5: HOME REMEDIES FOR CATS
(A SPECIAL CHAPTER BY DR. STEPHAN GRUNDY, PH.D., MASTER HERBALIST)

Most of the minor ailments from which cats suffer can be treated effectively at home. This chapter is meant to give a swift overview of some of the most common problems that occur, and some treatment options to which you might resort either if the problem is not serious enough for a vet visit, or as a last resort of desperation if the vet is not available to you in a major crisis. If you have any sort of medical background, or even a strong educated lay interest in medicine, you could not do better than to get a copy of what our household calls "The Big Cat Book" – that is, The Cat: Clinical Medicine and Management (ed. Susan E. Little, Elsevier, 2012).

This is the basic veterinarian's guide to clinical cat care; we have seen our own vet check the same book when he wanted to be sure of something. It is, obviously, written for professionals in the field; many of the conditions described are not things you could diagnose or treat at home. Though being able to guess at the severity of a condition – or whether it might be one that the cat could share with other animals or even humans - by recognizable symptoms is useful in and of itself.

The Cat is not a cheap book, especially in hardback (and you want at least a paperback hard-copy, because you really don't want to find yourself trying to find your page on a Kindle or laptop outside in the barn while simultaneously managing to control an ill or wounded cat). It is, however, well worthwhile. Remember that cat metabolism is not like human metabolism; they are lacking in some liver enzymes that are crucial to us for metabolizing certain drugs.

Avoid using medications or herbs on a cat unless you know that they are safe for cats. Some simple human over-the-counter medications, such as paracetamol, are absolutely fatal to cats even at low dosage. Nursing kittens and elderly cats (above nine or ten, though individual conditions vary) are particularly vulnerable to overdose. In the former case, their liver functions have not fully developed.

In the latter, their kidneys and possibly liver are likely to have lost some degree of function – too little loss to be noticed by the cat or human may be enough loss to interfere with the processing and excretion of some drugs. The guideline, "Start low, go slow" is especially important for the older and very young cat, or the cat that is already known to have any sort of liver or kidney problems! However, it is useful and might be life-saving to know that some human antibiotics absolutely are the same substances given to cats for the same purpose.

Every GP's favorite go-to, Augmentin (500 mg ampicillin/125 mg clavanulic acid) is also the vet's favorite go-to (cat dose: 5 mg ampicillin/lb once a day; clavanulic acid is proportionate). Metranidazole (Flagyl) is another cat antibiotic (5-25 mg/kg 1-4x daily – GI conditions, including giardiasis; bone and dental infections), as are clindamycin (often used for bone and dental infections – 2.5 mg/lb twice a day up to 10 mg/lb once a day), doxycycline (treating Lyme disease, among other things; 2 mg/lb every 12 hours), and cephalexin (Keflex – 10 mg/lb once daily).

This means that if you have a cat infection emergency and no vet available, you still have a chance of saving your cat if you keep emergency human antibiotics around. Another human drug that is commonly seen in veterinary practice and particularly when treating cats is prednisone (also prednisolone and the related drug hydrocortisone). Cats have a much higher tolerance for steroids than humans do. Their dosage is normally 1 mg/lb/day, though a severe autoimmune condition (or severe acute situation) might require up to 3 mg/lb/day.

So a fair-sized 10 lb cat would get 10-30 mg/day. Human tablets most commonly come in 5 mg, 10 mg, and 20 mg. Steroids are given to cats short-term to help with inflammation from an acute respiratory infection; long-term for auto-immune diseases and other inflammatory conditions; and, in short, pretty much everything for which they're given to humans. A dose of prednisone or one of its equivalents given in time has saved no few cats (and humans) with serious acute respiratory problems.

While these are major drugs, with very significant side effects, and should not be handed out casually by people with no veterinary training. If your cat is dying of a respiratory condition at 3 AM with no vet access or even long-distance advice available, this might be a desperate enough time to try it. In extreme situations, cats can tolerate opiates. Usually these, properly formulated for weight and metabolism and possibly fortified with other cat-appropriate analgesics, will be supplied by your vet when needed. If you are ever in a late-night desperate situation where you have a cat in agony and no vet available. Cats can often take human opiates if these are not supplemented with other painkillers that are toxic to them.

This means that you can give your cat plain codeine, but you cannot give it Tylenol III, because the paracetamol will kill it horribly (do not even think about using paracetamol to euthanize cats. Sometimes euthanasia is the only humane option, but paracetamol is not a swift or easy death). Make sure that the opioid preparation does not contain paracetamol, acetaminophen, ibuprofen, or aspirin, all of which are commonly added to opioid-based medication.

These include proprietary formulations such as Tylenol II, III, IV (codeine-acetaminophen); Vicodin (hydrocodone-acetaminophen); Percocet (oxycodone-acetaminophen); Solpadeine and Solpadol (different strengths of codeine/paracetamol); and many others. There are fentanyl patches available for cats with long-term pain, but they should not use human ones, as it's not possible to moderate the dosage and release rate to take their metabolism and bodyweight into account. Oral cat dosage for some common human medications. Again: make sure there is no cat-killing analgesic combined with the opioid drug in the particular pills you have!

- *Codeine – 0.5-2 mg/kg (1 kg=2.2 lbs) every 6-12 hours. Again: make*
- *sure that there is no cat-killing analgesic combined with the codeine*
- *Tramadol – 1-2 mg/kg, 2-4x daily.*
- *Hydrocodone – 0.5 mg/kg up to 2x daily*
- *Oxycodone – 2.5 mg/kg, up to 2x daily*
- *Oral morphine – 0.5 mg/kg, max of 4x/daily*

Do cats show any sign of responding to the "placebo effect"?

No, cats have never demonstrated a "placebo effect" response. Therefore, homeopathy is largely useless in treating cats - or any other animals who do not maintain a strong personal belief in the principles and efficacy of homeopathy. In short, don't waste your money or your cat's health. In demonstrable medical terms, the best you can achieve for your cat here is nothing.

At worst, if you try to medicate the cat directly with a homeopathy product rather than just sprinkling that bit of specially-labeled distilled water or crushed neutral pill over its food in hopes that the placebo effect on you might make you feel as if you were doing something for the cat, you can cause detrimental stress. This does not, of course, apply entirely to anyone who is using a homeopathic preparation as a vehicle for sympathetic healing magic.

The little bit of distilled water was, indeed, once upon a time part of some water, of which a teeny smidgen was part of some other water, of which a teeny smidgen was part of some other water, the bowl of which was once clinked against a vermouth bottle so that a drop of your homeopathic preparation could be used to make a martini. This actually should work according to the theory of sympathetic magic, but is not generally accepted outside of the circles of supernatural practitioners and people who appreciate martinis.

The other possible justification for using homeopathy on a cat, either in addition to a medically effective treatment or because you can't afford a medically effective treatment (and are presumably making your own homeopathic preparations, because if you could buy those, you could afford something that would help your cat) is that, whatever your beliefs, prayer for a sick animal is one of those things where it's hard to go wrong.

Even were one an absolute rationalist, animals are pretty good at picking up on it when someone strokes them with love and good will. Of that peculiar dichotomy, where they view us as parent cats as well as possibly kittens, a cat (who will tolerate contact at all) who perceives that it is being protected by the parent, is a cat under less stress, hence a cat whose immune system will be more effective.

If you are religious and you pray and trust your god or gods, your cat will also pick up on that trust, and that alone could help the cat. Also, I am not the man to say that your god or gods are not going to help your cat when you ask. I have prayed for cats myself on many occasions; and I believe that my prayers were answered. You may or may not.

And if you believe in homeopathy, and don't let that belief keep you from also getting the cat real treatment, it is possible that you can exert at least an indirect placebo effect on your cat. One of the crucial tests for whether a new medication is worth bringing out is, "Does it perform significantly better than placebo?" Placebo is a real thing, but it's not the same in cats as in people. We go for whatever our symbols of medical authority are, whether the white coat and stethoscope or the big scary mask and Cape buffalo horns. They go for the things that hit their instinctive buttons, and if a cat trusts humans – especially if it has been handled from an early age – that cat will respond better to your care.

Home First-Aid Tools for Cats

For home first aid on your cats, there are a few things you will want to keep around:

Activated charcoal – in case of a poisoning emergency where it might be appropriate.

Antiseptic – betadine or diluted hydrogen peroxide (5%; sold in most pharmacies). If you see an injury on one of your cats, clean it up! Even if you can't bandage it, making sure the wound is clean will go a long way towards avoiding complications.

Bandages – sometimes you can put a bandage on a cat. Sometimes you can't. They're good to have around, anyway.

Buprenorphine – this is the opiate that works best and is most often used on cats. If you are lucky and your vet knows you well, you may be able to get them to give you a couple of cat doses to hold onto in case of midnight emergencies (or you may not, since it is also a human prescription opioid, albeit used primarily in withdrawal/addiction recovery treatments for humans, rather than as a drug of addiction – hence this might or might not be legal, and your vet might or might not be willing to do it).

Cannabis preparations suitable for cats – only where these are legal, of course, although CBD oil is legal nearly everywhere, and, even without THC, has sedative, analgesic, anti-inflammatory, and anti-seizure qualities.

Catmint – an excellent means of corralling, bribing, and distracting the cat while you do whatever you need to do to it.

Claw clippers – if you have to hold the cat (which may already be frightened and in pain) and mess with it for more than ten seconds or so, you'll want to utilize these first.

Cotton (heavy; or canvas) drawstring bag – an alternative to the towel "purrito wrap" when a cat must be immobilized or at least kept from tearing you up (see page 85).

Eyedroppers – necessary for administering liquid medications either orally or into the ears. And they're never around when you want them, so keep a few spares somewhere. You can also use a syringe (without the needle, obviously) in just the same way. Be sure to wash and sterilize eyedroppers after each use. You can use hydrogen peroxide or Betadine, as long as you wash it out thoroughly with clean water after sterilizing.

Elizabethan collar – also known as the "cone of shame", this is an adjustable plastic cone that goes around the cat's neck and theoretically keeps it from licking or chewing at an injury. Be sure that the cat actually can eat and drink with it on, or you'll have to remove it for supervised eating/drinking periods.

Razor – you may need to shave the fur around an injury in order to affix a bandage.
Scalpel (with sterile blade for each use) – while you will rarely need to use this unless you prefer draining abscesses to letting nature take its course, if you do, you will really need it.

Scissors – Small and sharp. A very common minor injury is the tag of torn skin hanging off a cat's ear after a fight. This is painful, annoying, and a risk for more severe tearing. If there is only a little bit of healthy skin holding the tag on, often you can quickly snip it with the scissors, and if you move fast, often the cat doesn't even react. If there is a lot of whole ear that would have to be snipped, and therefore also a good blood supply to the injured part, the cat will do better to have stitches. Scissors are also useful for removing matted fur or fur that is too contaminated to be worth washing, clearing an area for shaving/bandaging (you try using a razor on a Persian without clipping the region first!), and many other purposes.

Syringes – large and medium for general-purpose uses (feeding and medicating cats).

Thermometer – mark this to avoid confusion with thermometers for human use, as it is going into the cats' rectums. Be sure to wash and sterilize the thermometer after each use, as faeces are a very common means of disease transmission

Tweezers – for removing ticks, splinters, etc.

Vaseline or something of a similar ilk – for lubricating the thermometer.

MEDICATING CATS

Described in the previous chapter, can sometimes be a little tricky. The most effective way to do this is using a tablet or capsule: you sneak up behind the cat, grab it by the scruff of its neck and tilt its head back, and place the pill in the back of its mouth, then close its mouth firmly before it knows what is happening. This requires a certain amount of practice to do effectively. Otherwise, you may have to get someone to hold the Kitty Off Button and hang onto the cat while you pill it, or purrito-wrap the cat for the process.

Veterinary supply places (and vets, for that matter) usually carry small plastic "pill-shooters" which can be used in a slightly less traumatic (to you) manner for medicating a cat. Get the vet to show you the best way to do this. A cat may also be given liquid medication (such as tinctures or oils) via eyedropper in much the same way as it is pilled. If the cat is extremely resistant, crush the pill into powder; dissolve the powder in a small amount of milk or water (about 1 cc), pull it into a syringe or eyedropper, and use the above cat-control methods to shoot the liquid into the cat's mouth.

However, should you be in a situation of having to do this in an emergency, be aware that there are some medications which should or must not be crushed, either for cats or for humans. The reasons for this are: the medication was formulated for slow release through the GI system (crushing it may cause an overdose due to getting, say, twenty-four hours' worth of drug in the course of two hours); the medication is likely to be destroyed by the GI system unless it is protected by its original formulation; the medication will itself harm the stomach lining unless mixed with a buffer and released in a controlled manner.

Most of the latter, to be sure, are NSAIDS (aspirin, ibuprofen, diclofenac) which you won't be giving your cat anyway; but the first two issues need to be considered. If you have obtained the pills from the vet, ask the vet about crushing (if you're having to use a bit of leftover originally-human medication in an emergency, check the guidelines in that regard: if it is safe to break or crush for humans, it is at least reasonably likely to break or crush for cats).

The odds are that crushing a pill or sprinkling a powder directly into the food, unless it is a relatively tasteless medication or there is a lot of food to dilute it, will result in the cat refusing to eat it (this does not necessarily apply to whole-herb powders, but pharmaceutical meds tend to taste nasty). Hiding a pill in the food and hoping the cat will swallow it in the course of things, that doesn't happen often. Actually I've never seen a cat that couldn't eat the treat and leave the pill sitting alone in the middle of the bowl. Don't bother.

It is usually easier to medicate your cat topically with an oil- or butter-based compound. Their skin is highly absorbent; also, if they can reach the area, they will lick the stuff off anyway. This is why you do not want to smear a cat with any substance that the cat should not ingest. It will end up inside the cat unless you can keep an Elizabethan collar on it. Note that cats are more sensitive to alcohol than humans. If making your own herbal tinctures for cats, use glycerine; the extraction rate is less (you need more herb and/or longer time for the same potency), but it's better for the cat. A few drops of an alcoholic tincture daily are unlikely to cause your cat significant harm, but why take chances you don't have to?

Colloid Silver for Cats – Colloid silver is often recommended for a variety of uses, including veterinary. Very few of these have any evidence to support them. What colloid silver can do: it is an effective antiseptic, and particularly useful for impregnating bandages over large-area infection-prone wounds (burns, broad abrasions), or gently patting down the area with a damp sponge several times a day if it cannot be bandaged in a practical way. Colloidal silver may be at least helpful in irrigating infected wounds, although by itself is unlikely to clear the infection (but cutting down on the bacterial count and variety even somewhat may help the cat's own body do so, if the infection has not gone systemic. The fevered animal needs oral antibiotics).

Although it is not as effective as antibiotic ointment or drops, colloidal silver can be used (1 drop in each eye/4x daily) for cat eye infections. Even if only one eye is affected, there is a risk of transmission to the other eye, so a mild antiseptic is a good precaution. If the infection persists more than 3-4 days, or if the cat becomes fevered, listless, loses appetite, etc., it really does need actual antibiotics.

What colloid silver cannot do: cure a systemic infection through oral administration. No one even knows how much silver absorbs and how much passes out to make special silver kitty poop, let alone whether silver could do anything worthwhile as an antibiotic in the bloodstream anyway. Silver has no natural function in the feline (or human) body, which means that, unlike most other trace elements, supplementation will not improve health by compensating for an unsuspected deficiency. It is impossible for a mammal to actually be silver-deficient.

Excessive silver (and no one even knows what that would be in a cat) can cause various forms of organ damage as well as argyria (skin turns irreversibly blue-gray). So following advice that you give a cat or dog a teaspoon or two of colloid silver every day as a general prophylactic is definitely not a good idea. Small amounts orally once in a while probably won't hurt the animal; they just aren't particularly likely to do it any good. If you did give your cat a few doses of oral colloid silver for its flu – do not be alarmed, you probably did not kill your cat unless they were incredibly large doses. You may not have helped it much, but you probably didn't harm it.

COMMON CAT PROBLEMS

Abscesses: The outdoors cat is likely to get scratched by other cats, nipped by its prey, or otherwise have its skin broken in high-bacterial circumstances. The feline immune system is pretty good at walling off and isolating such infections, which leads to abscesses – pockets of pus which eventually either reabsorb or, more usually, burst and drain. This may occur naturally, or you may deliberately drain it. There are a variety of home remedies for purely localized abscesses, including:
  • Putting warm, damp cloths on the abscess to try and bring the infection to the surface. Do not use onions or garlic as you might for a human.
  • Pulling the skin away from (not pushing towards) from the infected area in hopes of getting the abscess to burst. The reason you do not push towards the infected area is that doing so can break the wall of the abscess and allow the bacteria to enter the bloodstream, causing a dangerous systemic infection.
  • Draining infected pus out of the abscess by the above method (wear gloves and use disposable rags for this)
  • Cover wound with antibiotic ointment (don't use too much as cat will lick this off)

• If cat is kept indoors, you can try and use an "Elizabethan Collar" around the cat's neck. This will keep it from scratching an abscess on the head, or chewing one elsewhere. Your vet should have these items in various sizes.

• Make sure cat has lots of fresh water and good food. Try to keep indoors until open wound is healed over, or has fully drained.

• If cat begins to show signs of listlessness, dehydration (see p. 79), lack of interest in food or water, does not respond when petted, the secondary eyelid begins to show, and/or the cat shows signs of a fever (when in doubt take it): rush cat to vet. We nearly lost one of our favorite cats who started showing some of these symptoms late at night after suffering what had seemed to be a small ordinary abscess from a superficial injury. Had we not rushed him to the vet at 2 AM, he would have been dead by morning. As it was, he lived many long and happy years thereafter.

• In an emergency (like a snow storm) you can try giving a cat doses of the human antibiotics listed above.

• When an abscess bursts or is drained, the region should be washed and swabbed with Betadine or diluted hydrogen peroxide to sterilize it as best as possible. A drop of garlic juice may be introduced to the abscess hole; Robert Tisserand describes using one drop of tea tree essential oil effectively in a drained abscess on a cat. Note that essential oils are normally not recommended for use on cats (more on this topic later). Unless the animal is actually fevered or appears to be generally ill – signs that the protective mechanism of abscess formation has failed to keep the infection from entering the cat's general system - antibiotics will not be required. If systemic signs of infection appear, the cat should be treated with antibiotics immediately. It's best to keep an eye on a cat that you know has an abscess, and watch for signs of "hiding behavior" or other signs of serious illness. Major infections from abscesses are rare in comparison to the frequency of the condition, but they can come on dramatically in the course of a few hours.

Arthritis: Both osteoarthritis (mechanical wear on the joint leading to damage and chronic inflammation) and rheumatoid arthritis (an auto-immune inflammatory disease of the joints) occur in cats, but osteoarthritis is far more common, especially in cats over five or so. While cats are not as prone to arthritis of the hips as many large dogs, they do suffer from it. Home treatment for cat osteoarthritis is, as for humans, often helpful in relieving symptoms and improving quality of life, though not curative. In fact, it is very similar.

A warm, dry environment is the simplest means of mitigating an osteoarthritis patient's suffering. Whether this means making the cat an indoor/outdoor cat who can sleep by the radiator, putting at least a mild heat source in an outbuilding, or making sure that there are well-insulated small cat-houses about, will depend on your situation and the cat.

An arthritic cat will be stiff and may have increased difficulty in jumping up on things. Make sure that the cat can still reach food and water easily. Your vet can prescribe anti-inflammatory/analgesic drugs which are formulated and safe for cats. As already mentioned: do not give your cat human non-steroidal anti-inflammatory drugs (aspirin, ibuprofen, diclofenac, etc.) or paracetamol; it is very easy to kill the cat that way. In fact, it's hard not to kill a cat by giving it a human NSAID.

Supplements which are anecdotally reported to work on cats (and humans) include: turmeric powder (1/4 tsp/day for a cat); fish oil (omega-3 fatty acids; avoid cod liver oil as it is too high in vitamins A and D for cats to take regularly. Cat dosage is 1 gr 2x/day if possible; fish oil capsules for humans, as long as they are not high in vitamins A and D, are fine for cats); and glucosamine (reported to aid in producing joint lubrication and relieving the friction due to osteoarthritic damage – cat dosage: 120-500 mg/day).

Cannabis, particularly high-CBD formulations, is increasingly reported as a safe and effective feline anti-inflammatory and analgesic (see p. 110 for suggested dosages). If it is legal where you live, it is one of the best things you can give your arthritic old cat. Flaxseed (or linseed, if you prefer) oil, while used in humans as a dietary supplement for arthritis, is not metabolized the same way in cats (or dogs), and therefore is not particularly helpful for them, though food-grade flaxseed oil is safe for cats in small quantities.

Ear mites: Ear mites are common, painful, annoying, and contagious. You generally know that your cat has ear mites when it starts scratching its ears incessantly and miaowing in pain as it does, or flinches away from having its ears rubbed.

Ear mites can be dealt with by simply emptying half an eyedropper of olive oil (or other food-grade vegetable oil) into each ear twice a day, for as long as it takes to get rid of the mites. The oil suffocates them without doing any harm other than temporary annoyance to the cat.

I advise getting someone else to firmly grasp the cat by the scruff of the neck (the "kitty off button") while administering the oil. Many cats can be snuck up on and oiled in one ear before they know what's happening, but very few cats will stay quiet and cooperate by the time you are dosing ear #2.

Fleas: Advantage (trade mark brand) and other made-for-cats flea products have done wonders in preventing fleas and ticks over the last few years. Unfortunately they can be expensive if you have a lot of cats. And cheaper dog products are not suitable for cats, I mean this, don't use them. Anti-pest products formulated specifically for dogs contain pyrethroids.

These are cheap, effective, and dogs are strongly resistant to this class of insecticide, more so than humans (although dogs can still suffer severe neurological poisoning in overdose, as when dog flea and/or tick medication is applied incorrectly). Cats are highly vulnerable to pyrethroids (pyrethrum, etofenoprox, allethrin, permethrin, sumethrin, and others – including all natural products that mention the pyrethrum plant (Chrysanthemum cinerariaefolium.

This is why you never, ever treat a cat with a flea or tick product that is formulated specifically for dogs! Getting it on yourself isn't a great idea either). What you can do, is buy large dog-sized bottles of products that are also used on cats (like Advantage) and measure out the proper amount for a cat using a syringe. Most vets can help you figure out the proper dosage, or just buy one large cat tube and one small cat tube of the original product.

Then measure from the larger bottles accordingly. Just make sure the formula in the dog-sized bottle is THE SAME FORMULA that is used for cats. This is a cat breeder's trick that was passed onto me by a breeder friend. Cat breeders, like barn cat owners, often have multiple cats to treat and find the single tubes of medicine prohibitively expensive.

If you still can't afford to treat all your barn cats, be sure to treat those who go inside your house, either as mouse chasers or part-time family pets. Otherwise, you are almost certain to have fleas inside your house. And be sure to treat any indoor cats you may have as pets, and limit their exposure to the outdoor cats if you can. There really aren't any very effective home remedies for fleas.

There are a few things that can be done to diminish the burden, such as dusting the cats, their bedding, and your floors with food-grade diatomaceous earth (and it has to be food-grade, because some of it will end up inside the cats as they groom themselves!), scattering dried flea-repellent herbs (pennyroyal, tansy, southernwood, lavender), etc.

We get the cats to treat themselves by mixing a good bit of dried catmint with food-grade diatomaceous earth and dried lavender, and spreading several handfuls of the mixture over the ground in a dry and pleasant place where cats like to lounge...Easiest way of medicating a cat I've found in nearly fifty years!

One caveat: do not use any herb that might be toxic to a cat, such as pennyroyal, tansy, or southernwood, as part of this mixture, because the cats will be eating it as well as rolling in it. But ultimately, commercial/veterinary treatments are the only way to really deal with a flea problem.

Flu: Cat flu is often the most devastating thing that can happen to a barn cat colony, especially if there are kittens (some survive, and a few become lifelong sufferers/carriers). Cat flu is characterized by a copious and often purulent discharge from eyes and nose, wheezy breathing, fever, lethargy, loss of appetite, and, if the cat is not kept warm, well-hydrated, and carefully tended, often death or lifelong ill-health.

When cat flu appears in your colony, the best option is to isolate the sufferers at once in a warm and comfortable environment where you can keep a close eye on them. Remember to wash your hands thoroughly immediately before entering and immediately after exiting the contagion zone. If it is possible to change the cat bedding, this should be done at the first sign of flu in the colony. As with humans, antibiotics are ineffective against the flu virus itself.

However, be aware that a severe case of flu may also, and frequently does, lead to a bacterial superinfection and bacterial pneumonia, which does require (and is usually effectively treated by) antibiotics. I consulted with our local vets on the issue of feline antivirals. There are antiviral drugs for cats, but these are generally reserved for serious chronic infections (feline herpesvirus, feline retroviruses) and seldom if ever prescribed for even the most severe flu infections. The vets recommended a general regime of immunity boosters.

Echinacea is safe for cats, and should be administered to the whole colony for ca. 2 weeks if possible if any of its members or the neighbors' cats show any signs of flu. Dried or fresh plantain (herbs of the Plantago species (greater plantain, ribwort plantain) can also be added to the food at roughly 1 tsp dry/3 tsp fresh herb per cat per day at this time, as a possible prophylactic or mitigator of the flu virus and as a prophylactic against bacterial infections associated with the virus-weakened system.

Hair loss: Many cats begin to lose hair as they get older, and most cats will shed more in the spring. Some breeds of long haired cats will drop almost all their winter coat at once, which can give the impression that they are ill. Hair loss caused by illness (or pests) tends to be patchy and leaves bald spots on the skin. The skin may turn red, angry and even become infected. Unlike dogs, it's not a good idea to bathe a cat with these symptoms, unless directed to by a vet.

If hair loss is light, try feeding the cat extra treats of meat, eggs and other good foods. If it continues or gets worse, a vet's advice is a good idea, since the cause could be any number of problems. A surprising amount of hair loss can be caused by flea allergies. The only cure for that is flea prevention. Use of a flea treatment such as Advantage is in order.

Steroids such as prednisolone are often prescribed for cats with hair loss because it is so often due either to allergy or to auto-immunity. It is possible that such a cat will only need its 'roids during intermittent acute attacks, especially if the trigger is external; or it may have to take them all its life. You may also want to consider re-homing a cat with a serious chronic hair loss condition, or reassigning it to "pet" status.

Male Reproduction [Prevention]: As discussed earlier (p.82) there really is not a safe and humane way (especially for someone without vet training) to neuter a male cat at home. Rubber banding does not work on cats.

Ringworm: Despite the name, this is actually a fungal infection, not a parasite. The typical markings – itchy, raised red rings around apparently untouched centers (though they may start as simple blotches) are not as noticeable in cats, but they quickly start losing fur and developing a scabby look, at which point the rings are usually perceptible. Normal treatment is by prescription, oral in cats and topical in humans (yes, you can get ringworm from your cat or vice versa).

It can also be treated by applying undiluted apple cider vinegar to the area and letting it dry (3-4x/day), and/or keeping the area covered with coconut oil (for humans, you can also add a couple of drops of oregano and lemon grass essential oils, but don't do this for cats). The latter may not work with all cats or lesion locations, as there is some risk that the cat will irritate the area further by licking. The apple cider vinegar is probably a better choice.

Skin rashes: These are not uncommon in cats, especially longhairs and especially if flea control is a problem – as is often the case with indoor/outdoor cats in the summer. The important thing is to keep the cat from scratching (damages the skin, introduces bacteria, risks serious infection), which means keeping the cat from itching.

This is one of the extremely rare cases where you can use an essential oil on a cat: both Roman and German chamomile are safe. Dilute 1:10 in a food-grade vegetable oil and spread a small amount over the affected area several times a day. This is particularly useful if the rash is of a dry and scabby nature. If you live where cannabis is legal and available, you can also make or purchase an infused oil to use in the same manner.

CBD oil without THC, which is more commonly legally available, is not as effective for dealing with itching and pain (although it will help some, and possibly a great deal), but is still a very good and cat-safe anti-inflammatory which can be applied topically and will continue to do the cat good when it licks the oil off. Remember that at this time, even in legal states, your vet is prohibited from prescribing or even recommending THC or CBD products for animals due to the lack of clinical testing. But if it is legal for you to use such a product, it is probably legal for you to give it to your cat.

Ticks: Cats can and do get ticks, which are a common problem in rural areas worldwide. Regular flea/pest treatments discourage them, but are not 100% effective (although they are an important risk reduction feature in areas where tick-borne diseases are endemic). Ticks are removed by grasping them with tweezers at the point where they enter the skin and pulling slowly, but steadily, straight out.

Be sure that you have removed all of the tick's head; if bits remain, they can cause nasty infections. DO NOT attempt to burn the tick in order to make it let go. This will only terrify and hurt the cat. Smothering ticks with petroleum jelly doesn't work either. They have to be manually removed. Note that, due to the risk of contracting disease, children should never remove ticks. If a cat has a large number of ticks, it is better and safer all around to take it to the vet for removal if possible than to try to do it yourself.

Keep cat isolated for a few days if you can (preferably in an outbuilding rather than the house) and make sure there are no signs of secondary infection. If cat is left outside, at least keep an eye on it for signs of "hiding" behavior, which could indicate illness. You can treat the tick bite area with small amounts of antibiotic ointment or cortisone formula.

Don't use too much, as cats will tend to lick it off and it's not supposed to be an internal medicine. If cat begins to run a fever or signs of illness, take to vet immediately. This may be an illness transferable to human beings, and you must find out right away. Most of the time there is nothing to worry about, but diseases like Rocky Mountain Spotted Fever or Lyme Disease make this sort of checkup necessary. Cats can get and transmit – not directly, but via their ticks - Lyme disease (*Borrelia burgdorferi*).

If you live in a Lyme disease-endemic area and have to remove a tick from your cat, note the date and keep a close eye on the animal for several weeks (including brushing the fur aside to see if any rash is forming). Any sign of not being well in this cat probably means a trip to the vet. Lyme disease can easily be treated with antibiotics and without long-term consequences if it is caught early. If it is not caught early, there is a risk of long-term consequences in both humans and cats even after antibiotic treatment.

Tooth and Gum infections: Seen occasionally, particularly in older cats. The cat stops eating dry food or will not eat; may paw at its mouth or cry softly; becomes defensive and ill-tempered towards other animals; flinches away violently when its mouth is touched. It may start drooling; its jaw may be swollen on one side. This cat is in terrible pain, as anyone who has had a severe toothache can imagine.

First, and immediately, it needs antibiotics and analgesia (the vet will most likely prescribe buprenorphine and/or an anti-inflammatory formulated specifically for cats). When the immediate infection has subsided, it is probably best for the vet to remove the offending tooth. Note that, while clove essential oil works surprisingly well for the acute pain of human toothaches, you cannot safely use it on a cat. A cat can live perfectly well with no teeth at all, so long as it is fed on wet food.

A nutritious cat-slop may also be made by blending cooked chicken meat with cooked brown rice, lactose-free milk or water, and a sprinkle of cat vitamins. Some of the best brands of cat food chiefly consist of chicken meat, brown rice, and a vitamin supplement.

If nothing else is available, dry crunchies can be soaked until they become mushy for this cat, even soaked in milk (ideally lactose-free or reconstituted cat milk) if it is reluctant to eat them soaked in water. The toothless cat can and will still hunt with all its old enthusiasm and the vast majority of its old skill. It can kill with its claws or sharp blows of its paws; and it can and will teach other cats the rudiments of hunting. It just can't chew crunchies – or eat the rodents it kills.

Urinary problems: These are particularly common in cats. They are particularly prone to kidney stones, often small ones which irritate the inside of the urinary tract (cat may have bloody urine, or, if a stone is large enough to get lodged between kidneys and bladder, bouts of major internal pain around its flank and lower back). Chronic kidney failure is one of the most frequently-seen causes of death in older cats. Keep an eye on cats that are drinking and urinating abnormal amounts, either too much or too little.

This can be a symptom of a number of things, including both incipient kidney failure and acute diabetes mellitus. Whatever it is, it probably isn't going to be good, and the vet needs to have a look at the cat if possible. Other signs of urinary trouble include: straining to urinate, making sounds of distress while urinating; excessive licking around the area; dragging the rump across the floor (this may also be a sign of worms), starting to urinate in unusual places with no obvious trigger, abnormally-colored urine (dark = hyper-concentrated; very pale = possibly passing straight through the cat without full processing, or a sign that the cat is abnormally thirsty; pink-tinged = blood; anything from an infection to major cancer; cloudy = pus); unusually strong-smelling urine (hyper-concentrated).

Unspayed females repeating the heat/traumatic intercourse/birthing cycle repeatedly are highly prone to lower urinary infections (near the opening), which, if they remain untreated, can move up to affect the kidneys and, if not treated in time, kill the cat. If you have kept your best huntress intact to replenish a high natural attrition rate with well-trained kittens, but she has more than two infections in this area over the course of three years – spay her and get another breeding queen.

The risk of keeping her intact with a problem that might easily migrate to become kitty pelvic inflammatory disease and/or kill her along with any litter she is carrying at the time is not worth her services as a provider of more cats, especially since she will probably continue to teach other females' kittens. Older males are prone to prostate hyperplasia – same problem any aul' fella can have, whether cat, dog, or human. The gland bulks up and blocks the passage of urine. Tom will be trying to urinate frequently, but not able to get out more than a little bit of a time.

If the condition isn't caught by this stage and the passage gets altogether blocked - if that bladder is not drained fast, there is a slow and hideous death about to happen. In short: when Tom is straining to widdle, take him to the vet NOW. Females are slightly more prone to contract infection, but the male feline urinary tract, though longer than the female's, is also narrower and more easily blocked by a variety of causes.

The most usual first-line treatment for urinary problems which do not require urgent and/or surgical intervention is antibiotics, since infections are the most usual cause. If the condition does not respond to antibiotics, this also suggests that it is not being caused by infection. Ca. 64% of Feline Lower Urinary Tract Disease (FLUTD) is idiopathic, meaning "cause could not be determined"; the other two major causes are infections and repeated bouts of stones.

Powdered cranberry is safe for cats (cranberry juice has too much sugar in it for them, and you try to get a cat to drink it, anyway!) and usually can be mixed into food without too much objection. Note that cranberry is a prophylactic that keeps E. coli (and possibly other bacteria, but E. coli is the one we know about) from adhering to the bladder wall, often the first stage in evolving an infection. It is not a cure for an existing infection. Stinging nettles are anti-inflammatory and diuretic, with a strong affinity for the urinary system.

Treating with nettle will probably not suffice to clear a severe or even moderate urinary infection, but may help mitigate it; and may also aid a cat to clear a mild urinary infection on its own. The older male cat with a tendency towards urinary problems is the one who is most likely to benefit from oral nettle treatment.

There is prescription cat food which encourages flushing of the urinary system (preventative against both infections and stones), usually prescribed to cats who have a history of urinary stones and/or repeated infections.

A kidney stone that is large enough to block a passageway requires urgent, immediate veterinary treatment. Aside from the excruciating pain that the cat will suffer until the stone is removed or passed, blockage of a urethra will mean that urine backs up in the kidney on that side, damaging and eventually destroying it. While a cat, like a human, can live with only one functional kidney, it may or may not survive the destructive process ravaging the other one.

Worms: Cats that hunt will get worms. Even 100% indoor cats get worms occasionally (tapeworms are transmitted by fleas). Barn cats with worms will not feel as healthy as worm-free cats and will not have the energy to hunt as well as they might. Also, worms can be passed on to humans (especially children), which is an unpleasant experience all around. So, worm your cats once or twice a year, if you can. Your cats will be better workers, and your family will be happier. Some areas have very high endemic levels of some worms, or the local worms are particularly persistent species (hookworm, roundworm), so specific prophylactic worming may be advisable more often. Ask your local vet for their recommendation.

Suggested minimal health care for barn cats is to give them worm medications once or twice a year. This is a lot less traumatic than it used to be. Most vets can provide pills that need only one or two doses to be effective. So you only need to do one or two barn cat roundups for mass pilling. Be sure to get cats back outside soon after you pill them. The pills work by pushing the worms out of the system via the most obvious route. Small children should not play with the barn cats for several days after pilling them, for the same reason.

Food-grade diatomaceous earth, given at ca. 1 tsp/day (average-sized 8-12 lb adult cat) for two to four weeks, is effective against roundworms, hookworms, whip worms, and pin worms. It is uncertain how effective it is against tapeworms, although there are anecdotal accounts suggesting that it may have some effect.

A commonly recommended natural remedy for cat tapeworms is 1 tsp finely crushed raw pumpkin seed mixed into the food daily for at least 3 weeks. I cannot vouch for how effective this might be, but if you have a lot of cats with worms and can't manage commercial medications for all of them in one go, it's probably worth trying. Turmeric powder (1/4 tsp/day) is also reputed to be effective against worms in cats and has shown good potential efficacy against other parasites as well. Curcumin is the active constituent, and there are curcumin formulations specifically for cats.

MORE SERIOUS CONDITIONS:

Cats can develop much the same range of health problems that humans do. Cats can become diabetic, hyper- or hypo-thyroid, or suffer from adrenal gland imbalances. They can develop the same cancers and heart problems that we do. Older male cats, most especially if not neutered, can suffer from all the same prostate problems that an old man endures. They are as vulnerable to allergies and immune-system diseases as humans are. However, the vast majority of such conditions require a vet to diagnose and treat.

The serious conditions that you are likely to both identify and be able to deal with in your barn cats are generally limited to physical trauma, possibly poisoning, and complications from the various simple, common conditions discussed in the previous section. The most important major health treatment: vaccination is the best way to prevent the major contagious devastating diseases among your cats (and other livestock, and family members).

Broken bones are usually best treated by the vet. Cats are noted for their excellence as orthopedic patients; their bones reunite easily and generally heal quickly and well; but professional stabilization of a fracture is by far best. The vast majority of cat bone fractures (over 70%) happen to a hind limb or the pelvis; 11-23% of those remaining are to the bones of face and jaw, usually from vehicular trauma or making a bad landing from a high fall (Harasen and Little, pp. 704-05).

The latter usually require veterinary reconstruction, although we once had an older rescue tom whose face had clearly been badly broken and healed functionally without the benefit of wiring. The likeliest major problem that you may face in a situation without 24-hour vet service and can also deal with at least on a very temporary basis is major trauma to a tail, hind leg, or paw.

This comes in several levels:

1) A broken bone is suspected, but the skin is not broken. Immobilize the limb; splint, if you can, as for a human with a similar injury: the object is to immobilize the joint above and the joint below the break. If the bone is visibly crooked, do not attempt to straighten it yourself if you have any hope of getting the cat to the vet; you risk doing even more damage that way. Note that a cat can walk, and do many other things, including run away and hide, on three legs. If the bone in question is a toe bone, there really isn't much you, or the vet, can or maybe even should do about it. If you have a little experience in bandaging cats, you could wrap the paw to keep it stable (being careful not to impair circulation in any way!) and perhaps apply a splint – which is just what the ER would do for you if it were your broken toe. Otherwise, keep the cat indoors if possible and keep a close eye on it until it is using the paw fully again. The two middle toes of each foot are the main weight-bearers. You may not even know it if your cat has a broken outer toe, unless the break is severe enough for the paw to be visibly distorted or you accidentally touch the injured spot. If a weight-bearing toe is broken, particularly badly broken, the cat may be unwilling or unable to walk on that foot.

2) Compound fracture – the broken bone has pierced the skin. This is generally considered a surgical emergency for a lot of reasons. If the injury is bleeding, stop it with compression (you will probably have to immobilize the cat first). Wash with antiseptic. Give painkiller if you have any cat-safe painkiller. Take the animal to the vet the moment you can. Unless you know what you are doing, do not attempt to move the bone back into realignment yourself. You will only hurt the cat more and quite possibly worsen the injury by damaging blood vessels and/or nerves, as well as increasing the risk of a severe infection. Do not use a tourniquet unless either blood is visibly pumping (means an artery has been breached) or the cat is obviously losing a lot of blood and you can't stop it. Then, better to lose the limb than the life, even for a cat.

3) Total severance – the tail or paw is gone. Clean the wound, stop any bleeding, and bandage. The vet will probably have to stitch up the skin over the stump, as exposed bone is a chronic gateway for infection, and may need to remove damaged bone and damaged/dying/severely infected tissue at the site of the injury as well.

4) A paw or part of the tail is hanging off/completely crushed: the bone has been completely severed, and the injured part is attached only by a bit of skin and a few shreds of flesh. This is probably the most stressful form of amputation injury for you. Clean the wound and make one quick cut with your sterile scalpel or sterilized sharp scissors to remove to remove the partially-severed area (if it looks as though more than one quick cut will be required and the limb below the severance point is relatively intact, the vet might be able to save it, so immobilize in position as gently as you can and leave the whole issue for the vet). Make sure the bleeding is stopped.

Get the animal to the vet as soon as you are able. Remember that, although cats have been known to heal with their skin and flesh retracting a bit from exposed bone – and sometimes the bone just does dry up and fall off - that stump may well continue to be a problem as long as it is not covered by healthy skin, and sooner or later it is likely to need to be professionally dealt with. Especially if it's a tail, because you do not want that infection going up the cat's spine to its brain, which is a very real risk.

A cat without a tail can adjust quickly to the change in its balance – as, surprisingly, can a cat with only three legs. There has been many a "Stumpy" or "Gimpy" who successfully continued a fine career as a hunter – some of them without ever receiving human assistance for their injuries and recoveries. So the loss of a tail or even a leg is no reason to put down a cat, even if that cat is totally a semi-feral working cat. Neither its hunting effectiveness nor its quality of life will be compromised noticeably by the missing part.

Poisoning: This is, unfortunately, a common killer of barn cats. Some poisons that are eaten by rats or birds remain lethal when the cat has killed and eaten its weakened prey; there are also various opportunities for accidental poisoning on a farm (weedkiller, antifreeze, etc.). The first thing to do when you suspect a cat has been poisoned is to identify the poison if you can, and call your vet or veterinary poison control center. Many antidotes are specific to their poisons: for instance, the coumarin-based rat poisons which are particularly common are counteracted with a shot of vitamin K.

It might be wise to ask at your local farm store about popular rodent poisons, toxic seed grain treatments, and so forth, so that you can find out what the symptoms of the likeliest types of poisoning in your area are. Activated charcoal is less often used in humans than was previously the case, but still plays an important role in treating many forms of animal poisonings.

However, it is not recommended: in most cases when the animal is showing obvious symptoms (means the toxin has already been absorbed); for small organic molecules and alcohols (ethanol, xylitol); with corrosive or caustic toxins. Activated charcoal is usually most effective in the first hour after the poison was ingested: it works by neutralizing the toxic substance directly in the GI system. Some slower-releasing or slower-metabolizing poisons may require multiple doses over a period of time.

To dose a cat with activated charcoal, it must be mixed into water in a syringe and dripped into the cat's mouth a bit at a time, making sure each mouthful goes down before more is given. The dangers of activated charcoal are: vomiting (not necessarily a bad thing; your vet may administer an emetic as well); aspiration pneumonia (a very bad thing, caused by liquid going down into the lungs and leading to infection); and electrolyte imbalance (hyper-natraemia, or excess sodium – make sure the cat remains well-hydrated).

Small animal dosage of activated charcoal for neutralizing poison is 1-5 mg charcoal/kilo of bodyweight. If your vet advises making the cat throw up, 3% hydrogen peroxide at 1 teaspoon (5 ml) per 5 lbs (slightly under 2.5 kilos) will achieve this quickly.

With some poisons, your vet may also recommend the use of a cathartic (moves substances more quickly through the GI system, diminishing absorption) such as sorbitol, which is frequently pre-mixed into activated charcoal solutions for animals. The cathartic dose of sorbitol for cats is 3 ml per kg (2.2 lbs).

Basic Herbal Remedy Making

Infusion – an infusion is usually approximately a handful of fresh herb or a third-handful of dry in 1 cup (almost 250 ml) of boiling water, covered to discourage volatile escape and left to stand for at least 15 minutes, then strained.

Oil or butter – to make an oil for treating cats, you need to start with a food-grade, cat-safe oil. Using a covered double boiler (if possible), simmer 1 part herb (by volume) to 3 parts oil. The herb should be crushed to powder if dry, or chopped finely if fresh, to allow for maximum absorption. The covering of the pot discourages loss of volatile components during heating. The oil should simmer at a very low temperature for 6-12 hours.

Medicinal herb butter is made in the same manner. If the herb in question is fresh cannabis, it should be dried in the oven for 1 hour at ca. 100 C/212 F in order to activate the cannabinoids before the infusion process is begun. If you have more time and are using an oil which is liquid at room temperature, you can make an infused oil by combining the same proportions and simply putting the bottle in a dark place to steep for 2-4 weeks before straining. If the herbs are fresh, be sure to wash them well, with soap, before chopping: olive oil, for instance, is often inclined towards mold colonies.

Allowing as little oxygenated "head space" in a storage bottle, and keeping it in a cold place after it has been strained, will help too. Do not use a moldy oil or salve. Coconut oil is solid at room temperature, but melts easily, making it particularly convenient for topical applications. Oral coconut oil has not been demonstrated to have any significant benefit for cats, but it does not seem to pose any danger to them. Coconut oil has some anti-fungal activity and may be the best choice as a base if you have to medicate a fungal condition such as ringworm with a home remedy.

Ointment – making an ointment uses the same principles and proportions of extraction as making a hot-method oil: heating the herb and the extraction media very gently for a long time. The only difference is that you add beeswax or food-grade paraffin to melt into the mixture until, when a few drops are cooled on a surface, it has achieved the consistency you desire. If it is too soft and oily, add more beeswax. If it is too stiff, add more oil.

Poultices and Compresses – in practical terms, what you apply to a cat in this regard is a lot more likely to end up as a compress than a poultice. A compress is held onto the affected area for a matter of minutes, a poultice is supposed to be there for as much as a few hours, but convincing the cat of that is your problem. In either case, the basic idea is to apply heat and/or medication directly to an affected area. Common conditions for which poultices or compresses are used are abscesses (the heat helps bring the abscess to a head so that it can be drained), sprains, arthritic joints; it is rare to use them for respiratory conditions in cats, though not uncommon in human.

The simplest form of compress is a pad of clean cloth that is soaked in hot water (no hotter than you can stand to plunge your fingers into for at least a minute – you don't want to burn your cat!), wrung out, and held against the affected area for ca. 5-10 minutes, or as long as the cat will have it. A hot water bottle, wrapped in a towel, will achieve much of the same goal and possibly be better tolerated by the cat (if you need to fully wrap a limb, just fill the rubber bottle ¼ of the way or so).

A herbal/medicated poultice is most easily made by either soaking crushed fresh herb in boiling water on a pad of clean cloth, letting it cool to tolerability, and applying it; or mixing dried and powdered herb into a stiff paste with hot water and either smearing on the area under a light bandage, if you think the cat might keep it on, or holding it on as a compress.

Tincture – A tincture is made by steeping herbs in ethanol (human-safe drinking spirits – never use any alcohol that you wouldn't at least theoretically put in a cocktail for yourself if you drank!) or glycerin ("maceration") for ca. 6 weeks to 2 months. Crush or chop the herb as finely as possible; pour the tincture medium in to cover it. Seal, shake and put away in a dark place; shake once a day.

If you are concerned about giving your cat an alcohol-based medication: add an equal part of boiling water to each dose and allow to cool before administering. This will steam off a significant part of the alcohol while not impairing the medicinal efficacy. Since the alcohol is necessary in part to preserve the medication in storage, no more than one dose at a time – or at least one day's dosage, if administration is divided – should be steamed off.

Food-grade glycerin is safe for cats to ingest, though it contains no nutritional benefits for them. While cats can tolerate very small amounts of alcohol, glycerin is a safer tincture medium for them. The one downside is that you may need to repeat the extraction with the same glycerin to make the tincture stronger after the first six weeks of maceration, as glycerin does not normally extract as efficiently as alcohol does.

HERBS AND OTHER MEDICATIONS WELL-TOLERATED BY CATS

Calendula or Pot/Cottage/English Marigold: (*Calendula officinalis*; not to be confused with the unrelated African marigold, *Tagetes erecta*) – an excellent herb for topical oils and creams to use on wounds, rashes, skin infections, and the like; safe when the cat licks it off. It has at least some antimicrobial function with topical application, including anti-fungal effects (and therefore might be usable if pharmaceutical ringworm treatments weren't available). Calendula also has anti-inflammatory and possibly mild analgesic qualities, so may be a useful topical treatment for a cat with arthritis or allergy problems.

California Poppy (*Eschscholzia californica*): Although this is a poppy, it is not an opium poppy and contains no opiates. It does, however, have sedative, calmative, and mild to moderate analgesic properties (might be a good herb to give in circumstances where you would give a human a dose of aspirin or paracetamol). While some lists of "plants poisonous to cats" include this herb, it is commonly found in veterinary herbal remedies. For small animals, both dogs and cats, Veterinary Herbal Medicine advises 25-400 mg/kg of the dried herb; for an infusion, 5-15 grams dry herb per 1 cup (8 oz, roughly 250 ml) water administered at ¼ to ½ cup total daily per 10 kg. For an ethanol tincture made with a herb/alcohol ratio of 1:2 to 1:3, the daily total is 0.5-2 ml per 10 kg. All daily doses are ideally divided into three parts for administration ca. every eight hours or as close as is reasonable (Wynn and Fougere, p. 504).

Cannabis sativa: If you live in a region where cannabis is legally available, you have probably wondered about using it on animals. At this time (2019), because few or no clinical studies have been done on cannabis in animals, your local vet cannot legally advise you to use it on your cat, let alone recommending or prescribing it, and still keep his or her license. You, however, are free to administer legal herbal products to your own animals. Having said that: cannabis is as non-toxic as a plant will ever get, and cats are almost notorious for responding enthusiastically to this particular herb.

It appears to affect them much like cat mint, and some cats approach their human's stash in a very similar manner. While it is highly important to minimize the psychoactive effects of THC in animals such as dogs or horses, which may very easily become disoriented and distressed, this does not seem to be an issue with cats (Nature's furry little stoners) to nearly the same degree.

It should also be noted that if your cat appears to be distressed or over-intoxicated, CBD specifically works to counter the psychedelic/psychoactive effects of THC, so a cat who has had more than it likes may be safely dosed with CBD oil to mitigate the psycho-activity. However, at least in humans, CBD is biphasic: low to moderate doses are not sedative and may be slightly stimulant, but high doses of CBD do have a sedative effect and will probably not wake up a cat that has passed out from high THC-dosing.

Informally, cannabis (particularly high-CBD formulations) has been effectively used to control seizures, inflammatory conditions such as osteoarthritis and auto-immune diseases, pain, and emotional distress in cats. I do use CBD oil (legal where I live) for my own cats, and would not hesitate to use a full-plant product for any of them, with the possible exception of a pregnant queen (full safety of THC in pregnancy not yet established – probably harmless, but not certainly so). An excellent guide to cannabis dosing and usage in animals is Gary Richter's *Ultimate Pet Health Guide*. For most chronic conditions, it is commonly recommended to start with around .5 to 1 mg THC and the same amount of CBD per day for an average 8-9 lb. cat.

5 mg/kg per day (about 20 mg for that 8-9 lb cat) may be a threshold dose for seizure control in some cats.

To work this out for dosage: 1 gram of dried high-quality cannabis flowers at 20% THC = 200 mg, or 200 starter doses for an 8 lb cat. Say that you infuse that gram of flowers in approximately 200 ml (0.85 cups American) of your medium (spirits, butter, oil). The measurements will not be as exact as in a pre-made product – you probably won't get every molecule of cannabinoid out of the plant material, and you probably will have some loss of the medium in the straining process - but they don't have to be for this particular drug, given its immense therapeutic index. Giving your cat a few milligrams extra with each dose will not put it at any risk, and you can safely increase the dosage slowly if it seems insufficient.

In the above example, anyway, you will not be worryingly wrong if you estimate 1 ml of the final product as roughly 1 mg THC, plus whatever the corresponding CBD percentage of that strain gives you (2% CBD – your 1 ml would have 1 mg THC and .1 mg CBD, which means you might want to add a pure CBD product). Many strains with a more balanced THC:CBD ratio are available in legal areas from dispensaries and, where permitted, as seeds for home-growing.

If you have reason to think that your cat needs a larger dose for medical purposes than is easily tolerated by the animal in a psychoactive sense, and you have access to fresh cannabis or its extracts, you may wish to consider using fresh instead of dried/decarboxylated herb. The THCa which is transformed into psychoactive THC by decarboxylation is still useful for the vast majority of the purposes for which you are giving it to your cat in the first place – it still works well in the peripheral nervous system, but does not seem to enter (or register on) the central nervous system where psycho-activity happens.

The best way to administer the fresh herb is to make a slow-infused oil (no heat; only a minute amount of THCa will be decarboxylated over the infusion time) or tincture; if this is something that you might be giving the cat several doses of a day, you definitely want to either make it a glycerin tincture or be particularly careful in steaming off the alcohol content before each dose. The most effective way to administer cannabis to a cat is by means of infused butter or food-grade vegetable oil. Oil can be given directly into the mouth by eyedropper, assuming that the cat will let you do this; oil or butter can be put on the paws for the cat to lick off, or rubbed into the inner surface of the ears where the skin is thin and absorption is swift.

Cats can receive the benefits of cannabis through inhalation, and we have known cats in partaking households that were in the habit of climbing into a smoker's lap and shoving their muzzles into the face to catch the exhale – but breathing smoke is no better for cats than it is for humans, and one should not encourage the cat to do this. It might be possible to dose a cat in the same manner by the much safer means of vaporizing. Some cats will drink a tiny bit of cannabis butter melted into milk (definitely go with the lactose-free if you can). Some cats will take one whiff and turn up their noses. The same is true for most methods of administration involving the cat's personal flavor judgment.

Cannabis dosage for pain relief, etc, is essentially "as seems to be required", since you cannot actually poison your cat with an overdose. Do keep in mind that cannabis in oil or butter taken orally comes on slowly and requires ca. 2 hours to reach peak, so if the cat is not achieving relief in half an hour, don't stuff more and more down it, or you will have a very limp and sleepy cat for a day or so. Keep in mind that it is also possible to completely knock your cat out for a very long time – over 24 hours – if you give it an extremely high dose. An animal which is unconscious for more than 6-8 hours or so, especially one that has already suffered a trauma where the very high analgesic dosage was indicated in the first place, will probably need fluid support, ideally by means of IV, although you can also carefully trickle liquid down its throat.

A cat who is unconscious for more than a day may also need protein support. You should definitely avoid giving a heavy anaesthetic dose to a cat who is going to be put back into or have access to the wild. They may fall asleep before they can find a place that is safe and warm, or they may suffer serious dehydration before you can find them. There is no guideline on the full anaesthetic dosage for a cat.

However, in both cats and dogs (which have an unfortunate tendency to eat large amounts of cannabis-chocolate products, risking death by chocolate poisoning), the dosages anecdotally reported for animals which have required veterinary or special attention after cannabis ingestion are consistently estimated as very considerably more than a human would use for recreational purposes (the high end of that is usually ca. 100 mg THC at a single dose; some people can, of course, tolerate or medically require more). Remember that oral tinctures (ethanol or glycerin) are more rapidly absorbed and are also metabolized out more rapidly than butter- or oil-based preparations!

How to make an oil- or butter-based cannabis extract:
Leaves, flowers, both, and/or various resin preparations can all
be used. If starting with whole fresh plant: dry in oven at ca. 100
C/212 F for approximately 1 hour (this converts the THCa and
CBDa into their active forms).

For oil or butter: crush the dried plant as finely as you can.
Mix at ca 1 part (by volume) cannabis to 3 parts oil or butter.
Ideally, this should be gently simmered in a double boiler or
crock pot, or at least very gently simmered, for approximately 6
hours. Decarboxylation has mainly happened already; what you
are doing with the gentle heat is speeding the absorption of the
cannabinoids into the medium with minimal loss of medicinal
constituents. If you are using relatively pure resin (hashish) or a
concentrate, these can both be dissolved straight into butter and
oil.

If you know the approximate THC and CBD contents, you can
actually work out dosage quite easily as well as safely (mainly
because you can't actually give an unsafe dosage), and titrate
up how much you give your animal until the desired effect is
achieved – think of starting with ca. 5 or 10 mg THC/dose, then
going up or down by effect. If you don't know the approximate
cannabinoid contents, go for about a 1:10 by volume for most
hashish, or 1:20+ by volume for a "hash oil", "shatter", "budder",
or "rosin" concentrate, which is extremely powerful.

If in doubt as to what your best option would be in terms of
what strain or subtype to purchase, ask at your dispensary. They
will know which strains they carry that are best for pain relief of
various types, psychoactive effects, and so forth. They may also
have pre-made oils of tested dosage which you can purchase and
apply directly to your cat.

Catmint (*Nepeta cataria***) or catnip:** Is so well-known as to
require little introduction. It serves cats for recreation, mood
improvement, and quite possibly as a mild to moderate painkiller.

Chamomile: Both German chamomile and Roman chamomile
are extremely non-toxic for cats or humans. Their essential oils
are the only ones that can safely be applied topically to cats under
most conditions, although I would still recommend a 1:10 dilution.
However, even if the cat licks it off after application, it will not do
any harm. In cats, as in humans, chamomile is calmative and also
aids with digestion.

Echinacea: This herb is safe for cats. Its effectiveness as a general immunity booster is uncertain in humans and unknown in cats; but it does show action against common respiratory viruses and seems to mitigate both the length and severity of, for instance, flu infections. It is most effective when administered at or shortly after the time of infection; it is strongly indicated for all cats in a colony if one of them is showing flu symptoms.

Eyebright (*Euphrasia officinalis***):** Is a very benign herb which pretty much does what it says on the tin. It is primarily used for eye infections or inflammatory conditions and the "ooky eyes" commonly appearing in association with cat respiratory illnesses (most often cat flu). Eye bright has mild antibiotic and good anti-inflammatory functions in both cats and humans.

The normal means of administration is a drop or two of a cooled infusion (perhaps with plantain and goldenseal also added for their antibiotic properties) in each eye, several times a day if the cat will stand for it. A glycerin tincture can also be mixed with plain water and a tiny bit of salt (1 cup/8 oz/250 ml water to 2 tablespoons/60 ml glycerin tincture to ¼ teaspoon/1.25 mg salt), and a couple of drops put in each eye several times a day.

Do not mix more than one day's dosage at a time, as under a 50% concentration, glycerin e ceases to be relatively microbe-free. Remember that, unless your vet specifically tells you otherwise: when treating one eye, you also want to treat the other one to prevent cross-infection. And you absolutely must make sure that your applicator has been sterilized each time before use, then treat the good eye before the bad one, to avoid spreading the infection to the other eye yourself.

Goldenseal(Hydrastus canadensis): A herb with good antibacterial and anti-inflammatory effects which is safe for cats. An infusion, tincture, or cat-edible ointment can be used topically in place of a commercial antibiotic ointment; adding plantain (*Plantago major/lanceolata*, below) to the mix can only help. Cool infusions of goldenseal (+/- plantain and/or eye bright) can be gently dropped into ooky eyes to help clean and clear them.

Internal dosing for an adult cat is: under 10 lbs (5 kg) – up to 1/8 tsp powdered herb once a day/less than 1/4 cup infusion or 1-3 drops tincture 1-3x a day. 10-20 lbs – 1/8 to ¼ tsp powdered herb daily; ¼ cup infusion or 3-5 drops tincture 1-3x/day. For short-term use only. Do not use this herb on newborn kittens or puppies, as it can cause brain damage in them. It is safe to use on older kittens or puppies, but cut down the adult dosages by weight.

Nettle: In cats as in humans, the common stinging nettle is an excellent and safe general tonic. As mentioned above, it is diuretic and anti-inflammatory, making a good adjunct (though not a cure) for treating urinary infections. It may also reduce some prostate-related urination problems (this is still uncertain in both humans and animals). Whether this is the case or not, the diuretic, tonic, and anti-inflammatory effects (with particular affinity for the urinary system) are all likely to be of benefit to the older male cat in particular, especially if he has any tendency to develop stones. Nettle can be administered dried, as an infusion, or as a tincture.

Plantain: Not the banana-like fruit, but the herb. The main two species are *Plantago major and Plantago lanceolata*. Both of them grow in grasslands and disturbed or waste areas almost everywhere that Europeans have settled; sometimes P. major (greater plantain) is called "White Man's Footprint".Both of these plantain species are active against Gram-positive bacteria, which includes two of the most common culprits in skin and wound infections: the Staphylococcus and Streptococcus species. They may also serve as topical anti-fungals.

They are considered medicinally interchangeable; the English-speaking world has historically preferred *Plantago major*, but *P. lanceolata* is more often used in Europe for pharmaceutical preparations due to higher percentages of active constituents (Vermeulen, pp. 231-32).

In humans, plantain is used externally for skin infections, insect bites, allergic rashes, and fungal infections; internally, it is used as a mild general anti-microbial, and particularly recommended by the British Herbal Pharmacoepia in cases of bloody cystitis (combines astringency and pro-coagulant action to minimize internal bleeding, and diuretic qualities which help keep the bladder flushed and cleaned – though remember that bloody urine could be from a simple bladder infection, or it could be a sign of advanced urinary-system cancer).

It may help to mitigate some viruses, clear chronic bronchitis, and aid in treating some respiratory and GI infections. The internal uses of plantain have not been tested on cats, but we at least know that the herb is safe to feed them. Fresh plantain leaves can be juiced (recommendation is ca 1 tsp juice/cat), chopped finely into cat food to see if they'll eat it, or made into an infused tea (large handful of chopped leaves in 1 cup of boiling water, steep at least 15 minutes) and mixed into a cat's food.

Dried plantain leaves can be crumbled into wet food, powdered and given to the cat inside a small gelatine capsule, or made into an infusion (use about 1/3 the amount of dried leaves that you would use fresh). If you have the opportunity to apply a poultice to a cat's infected wound or abscess, plantain is a very good choice. The infusion can also be used to wash a wound, although it is probably inferior to Betadine or diluted hydrogen peroxide. Plantain can also be made into an oil or salve, as long as you are careful to make sure that all ingredients are cat-safe. Do not confuse these plantains with the "plantain lily" or hosta, a common type of ornamental plant which is quite poisonous to cats!

Silver vine (*Actinidia polygama***)** – the traditional "Asian catnip": Often attractive to catnip non-responders as well as catnip lovers. The fruit galls seem to be the most highly favored part. The wood, leaves, etc. are often utilized in cat accessories, but are less powerful in terms of attraction and effect. Silver vine is used very much like catnip, and is non-toxic and non-damaging to the cat. Whether the traditional human benefits ascribed to this herb are relevant to cats (and how effective they are in humans) is unknown. At any rate, silver vine as a cat treat has recently made it to the West and is now available in some pet stores and on-line.

Turmeric: Turmeric (and its primary known active constituent, curcumin) is safe for cats and not notoriously noxiously flavored - i.e., some will like the taste and some won't. It is mainly used as an oral anti-inflammatory (powder: up to ¼ tsp/day), particularly for cats with arthritis and incipient arthritis; as a de-wormer (efficacy uncertain; dosage up to ¼ tsp/day); and as a general health tonic (ca. 1/8 tsp/day). Turmeric powder can also be put directly on a wound or superficial infection, and is completely safe when the cat licks it off.

One thing to be aware of: if you use turmeric powder topically on a black and white cat, you will have a calico cat for a while. If you use turmeric powder on a cat who lives indoors, you may have a calico house for a while. It's truly amazing what a powerful dye it is. If properly stored (airtight container and desiccant in a cool or cold dark place), turmeric powder can last up to three years from the time of grinding.

The chances that most turmeric was properly stored during shipping and while waiting in the shop are fairly minimal. Poorly stored turmeric may not remain medically useful for much longer than six months from the time of grinding. There are also some concerns about contamination of spices, particularly imported bulk spices. Neither of these things should necessarily discourage you from using turmeric on your cat; but you do need to be at least a little careful about the quality if you're using the plain powder rather than a pre-made cat-supplement. Fresh turmeric can be used directly on cats, both topically and (if you can get it into the cat) orally.

Valerian: A sedative in humans, valerian actually acts as an initial stimulant and slightly longer-term relaxant in cats. They respond to it much as they respond to catnip, and most cats are very enthusiastic about the scent. If aggression is a problem in your cat colony, dosing the primary culprits daily with a bit of valerian may well help and certainly will not harm or distress them, especially if they are among the majority who love it. Valerian works by the same mechanism as diazepam and other benzodiazapines (such as Valium), and one small study found that valerian + ketamine was more effective than diazepam + ketamine for cat sedation (Kaffashi, Kayat, and Mahmoudi).

Herbs and other medications not to use on cats: This is by no means a complete list. Never assume that, because a herb or medication is safe for a human or dog, it will also be safe for a cat. They have very different metabolic and digestive processes than humans (or dogs, which are actually omnivores with strong carnivorous tendencies, as opposed to cats being obligate carnivores), and this means that many things which are innocuous in a human are, at the same proportionate-to-weight-dosage, potentially fatal in a cat. In short: do not give your cat a herb or medication until you have confirmed that it is specifically safe for cats. **DO NOT, EVER, GIVE CATS PARACETAMOL, ACETAMINOPHEN, OR IBUPROFEN**. They cannot metabolize these. One human-sized tablet of paracetamol suffices to kill an adult cat, miserably.

There are non-steroidal anti-inflammatory drugs which are specifically formulated for cats, and these are available through your local vet. Cats do not metabolize aspirin well and break it down slowly. Although they can tolerate small, infrequent doses (10 mg/kg up to an absolute max of 25 mg/kg, no more frequently than 1 dose every 48 hours), it is not the optimal choice if there are other alternatives. Willow bark and other herbs containing salicylic acid (the basis of aspirin) such as meadowsweet and feverfew, while useful mild painkillers for humans, are likewise slowly metabolized by cats. For all intents and purposes, these herbs are aspirin. If you must use one of them at all for your cat, and I don't recommend it, calculate a human dose down to cat weight, then halve it on the grounds that you don't know what proportion of salicylic acid is in your raw herb, and administer only once every 48 hours.

Aloe vera: is an excellent home medication for humans in many regards, but is relatively toxic to cats. If your cat has suffered a burn or has a skin condition for which you would consider aloe in a human, do not use aloe gel on it unless you can prevent the cat from licking the area by either bandaging or attaching an "Elizabethan collar", assuming that the cat is not one of the majority who can wiggle out of the latter. Use a chamomile infusion as a wash, or apply the essential oil (either Roman or German) diluted 1:10 in a food-grade vegetable oil. This is also a situation where colloidal silver liquid application may be helpful in preventing or limiting infection.

Alfalfa: contains a constituent, canavanine, which can interfere with feline protein metabolism, blood counts, and spleen function. Alfalfa also contains coumarins (prevent blood clotting – the same substance that gives us both warfarin and our commonest rat poisons). It should never be given to cats.

Arnica (*Arnica montana*): is a common first-aid herb for treating bruising, swelling, and inflammation in humans – topically! It is unsafe for humans (or anyone else) to use on broken skin. It is highly poisonous for both humans and cats if ingested. Because you can usually assume that anything that gets on a cat will end up in a cat, no arnica-containing product should ever be used on a cat for any purpose unless you can be absolutely certain that the cat, or any other cats who may be around it, cannot reach the medicated body part in any way.

Comfrey: is relatively safe for humans at normal doses, but contains alkaloids that can cause liver damage and failure in cats even at low dosages (and in humans if very large amounts are used excessively for a period of time)

Garlic: Onions, and other members of the allium family are not well-metabolized by cats. Giving your cat a bit of stew that has garlic or onions in them is unlikely to cause problems, but these herbs ought not be administered as oral medications (topical might be fine, but if you can get a cat to keep a smelly poultice on, you're a better cat-herder than I am). Too much garlic can lead to vomiting and sometimes even haemolytic anaemia in cats. This means that sprinkling powdered garlic in cat food as a general immune booster/prophylactic is a very bad idea, even though it might be beneficial to some other types of animal.

Pennyroyal: is extremely toxic to the feline liver. Neither the herb nor any concentrated form such as essential oil should ever even be used in cat bedding or cat-walked carpets, for flea control (the most common household use of this herb). Pennyroyal should never, under any circumstances, be fed or applied to a cat.

Pyrethrum (*Chrysanthemum cinerariaefolium*) – a common ingredient in natural insecticides, both for garden use and for use on dogs (also found, directly or as a synthetic analogue, in many commercial dog flea/tick remedies). Do not use on or around cats. If you use a pyrethrum or pyrethin analogue to spray your garden, lock the cats up until the spray has dried completely (also check the manufacturer's cautions). Also, don't let your kids play in the garden until it is safe again: pyrethin isn't much better tolerated by humans than it is by cats. Cats are extremely vulnerable to pyrethin and all of its natural and synthetic variants. As mentioned above, this is also why you do not use dog-specific flea/tick treatments on cats, ever.

Wintergreen: contains methyl salicylate, which is highly toxic to cats. Never use this herb or any product containing it on a cat.

Essential Oils: are generally toxic to cats, even when the herb from which they are derived is usually cat-safe. Essential oils are extremely concentrated, and cats lack certain crucial liver enzymes for effectively metabolizing many of their common components. It is safe enough to let a cat into a room where a moderate amount of essential oils are vaporized into the air (though it is recommended that the cat always have the option of leaving the room when it needs to). Essential oils should not be given to cats orally, and generally should not be used topically on them. Essential oils penetrate the skin barrier easily, and usually if you put something topical on a cat, the cat will convert it to an oral medication by means of licking.

The only exception to this rule is that an extremely minute dose of tea tree oil (1 drop) has been used by Robert Tisserand, one of the leading figures in essential oil therapies for many years, to successfully disinfect a drained abscess on a cat. In general, however, essential oils should be avoided in cat treatment. Unless specifically formulated for cats, concentrated herbal extracts of any type should not be used on them. Most herbs are safe in low to moderate dosages as whole plants.

In summary: while it is best to seek out professional health-care treatment for your cats if you can, there are many home treatments for lesser problems and extreme emergencies that are within your grasp. Get your vet's advice whenever you can, and, most importantly, pay good attention to your cats so that you can stop little problems before they become big ones.

IN CLOSING

It is my hope that this book will help to answer some of the most basic question about keeping a healthy, working colony of country cats. The partnership between humans and cats has worked well for us throughout the world, for thousands of years. As long as your barn cats get food, fresh water, shelter, basic medical care, and as much affection as they will individually tolerate, you can expect to keep a thriving and happy colony of rodent-control engineers – and often dear companions as well.

A Collection of Tales
-From the Cats of Kilmurry House-

Trolle's Tale: "What the hell do we do next?"

My associate Valkyrja and I were roaming the hall one night when we heard something squeaking and flapping over our heads. It smelled tasty and sounded interesting, so we chased it. Eventually I leapt up and snagged it with my claws. It fell down, but it was still alive and crawling around. We circled it. It smelled like it ought to be eaten, and it looked like a mousie with wings...but when we closed in, it reared back and made these noises. Still, we knew our duty – were we not cats? – and we tracked it down the stairs and in the hallway. Then we sat and looked at it. Then we looked at each other. Then we looked at it some more, thinking, "What the hell do we do next?"

Eventually our people came along. After the irreverent and ungrateful wretches finished laughing at us, they brought back my friend the Great Pumpkin. His big paws touched the floor, and the next thing we heard was bones cracking in his teeth. Our people took the very dead winged mousie away from him and gave him some chicken. It was interesting to watch, though I didn't quite see how he did it. So what? I'm the Queen of this House, and everything in it belongs to me! Even the mousies! And the winged mousies! Mine! All mine!

Prrrrr.

Ragnar's First Tale: "Love to eat them mousies..."

When my people first let my brothers and I outside, I knew it was time to start hunting for myself again. I was no longer a sick kitten, but bigger and stronger than I'd ever been. Then I saw it...a huge brown rat scuttling against the wall. It was more than half my size, but I didn't hesitate a second. I leapt on it from behind, driving my claws in and biting down on the back of its neck. It thrashed a second – and then it was dead! I settled down to my feast. It was nice to have a fresh warm rodent again after two months of cat food.

When I had finished off my favorite inner bits, I dragged the rest over for my brothers. They turned their noses up at it – didn't know what was good! – but I left the rest for my people. I didn't actually see them eat it, but they must have liked it, because they made much of me and gave me treats. After that, I settled into a good routine. Go out in the morning; catch a rat and eat what I wanted; sleep it off, and go looking for another, munching on mice whenever I saw them.

Sometimes my people brought me into their outbuildings to hunt. Once I sprang up and caught a rat as soon as my paws hit the floor. The rat was still twitching when I heard another rodent. I leapt for it, bounced off the wall, and caught it on the rebound. I always get my mouse. Mommy did start wrinkling her nose a little when she picked me up at night, and Daddy started referring to me as "Ragnar Mousie-Breath", but I suppose every dedicated artist must suffer for their art.

RAGNAR'S TALE: "I THOUGHT THEY WERE GOING TO EAT ME"

I was born in a wild cat colony. My mother (who was also my aunt) took good care of her litter. She taught us to hunt mice and bugs, crawl into rubbish bins and tear open plastic bags, and run and hide from those big barky things that want to eat us. We all had runny noses, and I grew up thinking the world was a blurry place – I could only see out of one eye, and the other had gunk in it too. But I could see food moving, and smell it, and I knew about running from anything strange. One day one of the human things put some food down.

It smelled so good, but I barely got a lick or two before they pounced on us. I was feeling a little weak and slow-moving, and one of them grabbed me by the tail and stuffed me into a box with my litter mates. They put us into one of those smelly metal things that squash us on the road, and we all cried, because we knew we were going to die. We stopped for a little while; then a human stuffed me into a different box, and into another metal cat-squasher. There was a box just like mine already in there, with two little toms, one just barely old enough to eat bugs. They didn't smell frightened at all, and I wondered if they were just too stupid to be afraid.

The humans let us out in their den, and I ran right under cover. If they wanted to eat me, they'd have a hard time of it! Once I felt a little safer, I sniffed the air more carefully. This territory belonged to an older queen, I could tell. Maybe these creatures weren't cat-eaters? The younger toms were running around with no cover at all.

The humans put down wonderful-smelling food and sat down with the little toms, petting and playing with them. They didn't try to grab me again, just made soothing noises, and eventually I fell asleep. After a few days, I was getting used to the good food. My eyes were clearer and I felt stronger, and even started teaching the two young lads some rudiments of hunting. And I discovered that the nests in which humans sleep are very warm and soft, especially when inhabited. I was home.

PRINCE MORDRED'S TALE: "I WILL RULE UNTIL I DIE..."

I was born in an Irish castle, meant to be a king tom from birth. I was the biggest and strongest kitten in my litter. Cat-Mommy didn't have much milk, so Human-Mommy had to feed us with a syringe every four hours, night and day. The other kittens all cried, but I knew the milk was good. I sucked down all Human-Mommy would give me. I grew up indoors with a long-haired tortoiseshell named Trolle.

We were only two doors away from the big toms who wanted to eat me and mate with Trolle. But when one of them broke in, I flew at him hissing and treed him on top of the table until the humans came to take him away. I was less than half his size, but he wasn't getting my queen! As soon as I could, I started marking my territory. My people took me to the vet shortly thereafter. When we moved to New Home, Trolle had to stay indoors, but I was allowed outside. There were other females now, and they all belonged to me!

Kittens appeared, and I knew they were mine, because my queens must have made them. Those big long-haired toms never dared to leave their runs to challenge me once I was full-grown! I teach all my kittens to hunt mice, and I protect them from all dangers, driving off other toms and strange dogs. I have ruled the yard for many years, and I have my queens – if none of them are in heat now, I'm sure one will be soon. I have my battle-scars. A dog got my tail, and I have plenty of scratches and bite-marks from defeated opponents. But I'm still strong and healthy, and I will rule until I die.

A PERSONAL ACCOUNT OF A STRANGE BIRTH

By: Linda Graves
Brown Brook Farm

**Photo provided by
Linda Graves**

We have a dairy farm, and our cats are mostly barn cats, although we used to keep one female house cat to "resupply" hunting kittens, when born in the house and handled young, they would always stay tame and thus could be cared for better in the barn, especially if they got sick or injured.

One winter evening, just at dusk, in 2005, our English Shepherd dog at the time, Lucky, became frantic and demanded to be let outside. When I opened the door, I could hear the sounds of a terrific cat fight in one of our barns.

I thought it was a bit odd that he was so insistent on getting involved, but that is a common trait in the breed. They consider themselves the guardians of everything on the farm, two and four legged, as well as "second in command".

It wouldn't have been the first time he broke up a cat fight, just because he considered that behavior to be rude! A few minutes after I let him out, he knocked at the door and I opened it, he surprised me by stepping back and allowing our neutered tom house cat to enter first. Part of the mystery was solved when I noticed Alien was bleeding from several tears and punctures. He was Lucky's special friend and he clearly somehow knew that he was in danger, hence his "rescue". What I couldn't figure out was why a long-neutered male cat would be fighting. We didn't think much more about it until 61 days later. Our tiny (4 1/2#, about 2 kilos) house cat "Emily" was pregnant with her third litter. Everything appeared to be normal, although I was expecting a large litter as she was huge.

I heard her in the dark hours of the night, screaming, but was exhausted from several nights up with cows calving, and it never occurred to me that she'd have trouble giving birth. She never had before. The next morning, I went up to the upstairs spare room where she had been "nesting", and found her with a very unusual litter. She had a tiny, silver gray female kitten which was normal sized for a domestic short-hair, and three of the biggest kittens I've ever seen, anywhere. The little female weighed just about 100 grams. The three males weighed 7 1/2 and 8 ounces (200-225 grams). We used to breed Akita dogs, and the pups from a 140# bitch weighed 9 ounces!

This was when we realized that whatever Alien had been fighting with that night 2 months earlier was likely the father, and certainly not a normal domestic short hair cat! We handled them from birth, and from the minute their eyes opened, they were very different from our normal kittens. Extremely precocious, very active and into everything. My son took one to his new apartment when he moved out, but had to return him after 6 months. The cat literally took his apartment apart! He'd open cabinet doors, empty the contents, remove the heavy couch cushions and drag them into another room.

They definitely weren't made to be indoor cats. At 1 month, the tiny domestic short hair female weighed 1#. The three crosses (or "legends" or whatever you guys are calling them) weighed 27 ounces. At 8 weeks, they'd reached 3#. And remember, their mother only weighed a little over 4#! We had one neutered and kept him as a house cat. His personality was fascinating, and he was able to spend as much time as he wanted outdoors, so he wasn't overwhelming like the one our son took for a while.

However, by 1 year old he was almost purely nocturnal, and already developing a "wild" streak. Not that he was a problem with people. He loved being petted and knew where the food came from. But he just had to be outdoors. By 3 years old, he was disappearing as soon as the weather warmed up a bit in the Spring, and we wouldn't see him for months. The first time it happened, we thought he'd been killed by a coyote or bobcat or whatever. Feral cats have to be tough and strong to survive for long in the woods and fields. But when the weather started cooling down in September, he showed back up, sleek and fit, obviously having done very well for himself. The next year, he did it again, but didn't reappear until mid-December, in the middle of a sleet storm.

He'd obviously remembered the warmth of the house, and I saw him peeking in one of the kitchen windows. But when I opened the door, he ran... I had to chase him down almost 100 yards before he finally stopped and let me catch up to him. Once I brought him inside, he was fine. But you could see he was restless. He went to the woods the following Spring, and we never saw him again. Oh, his final weight as a mature young cat was 16#, pure muscle.

LEGEND CATS

THE QUESTION OF BOBCAT/DOMESTIC HYBRIDS

A CONVERSATION BETWEEN JAY BANGLE & MELODI GRUNDY: Jay Bangle is a professional cat breeder of Bangle-Bengals and a cat show judge.

Jay Bangle: To date, NO proven bobcat/domestic cat hybrids have ever shown up. Dr. Leslie Lyons of Univ. of Missouri has never been able to locate any, nor really say why. Last time we talked (it was years ago), she felt it had to do with the bobcat sperm not being able to penetrate the domestic cat eggs for fertilization. That was merely speculation on her part (but seriously educated speculation!), as there was no money to do any research on the fact as to why something doesn't happen that actually should.

Pixie-bobs are merely "look alike" cats. Their bob tail is a version of the Manx tailless gene (not all Manx are completely tailless - only show quality ones. They run the gamut of full tail to no tail (rumpy) with everything in between (stumpy & the like)). PB have NO NON-DOMESTIC cats in their heritage - at all.

They are called "Legend Cats" by PB breeders (or used to be, back when they did think they were bobcat crosses). These were found cats that appeared to be part bobcat. Not one was ever shown to have even a smidgen of bobcat DNA. As I said in a previous e-mail, the bobtail mutation is the same as the Manx mutation. The polydactyl is no different than the Hemingway polydactyl cats in Florida.

Melodi Grundy: Honestly, I'm still not sure this is correct, I believe no one has FOUND Bobcat/domestic cat crosses but nearly everyone with a Barn in the US, especially in the South, North East or West, has had experience with them - my major professor in college was owned by one, as was my Japanese housemate in Mississippi" Melodi Grundy.

Jay Bangle: Yes. Very typical "Legend Cat" history. They were merely feral cats (a domestic cat that lives without the aid of humans), not a true "wild" species. Except for the Bobcat, New World Cats have 36 chromosomes. Old World Cats have 38. Bobcats *do* have 38 chromosomes; but for some reason do not hybridize with domestic cats. Could be that they are really New World cats and are distant enough from domestic cats that they just can't interbreed.

Melodi Grundy: I would state that the current theory is this is either a different species of cat and/or a cat descended from domestic cats that have gone wild over the last 500 plus years since the introduction of the European Domestic cat only instead of getting fluffy and snowshoe paws like either Norwegian Forest Cats or Main Coons, it evolved Bobcat-like characteristics.

Jay Bangle: If we're talking Old World, Scottish Wild cats are a close relative of domestic cats. They hybridize easily with domestic cats, and it is why the SWC is on such severe decline - even 1st generation males are fertile (like Wolf/dog crosses), so it's just too easy for them to interbreed with domestics, diluting the pure genome. There is some debate as to whether African Wild cats (*Felis Silvestris Lybica*) or Scottish Wild Cats (Felis Silvestris Grampia) are closer genetically. There are just very few examples of pure SWC (Scottish Wild Cats) to study.

Melodi Grundy: They adapted by becoming mostly brown ticked and black striped tabby cats with short or no tails, giant back legs (for leaping), and look like Bobcats because that was physically adaptive in the Southeastern US and allowed competition with Bobcats, Maine Coons and Lynx in the Northeast and Western forests?

Jay Bangle: Form follows function. Cats are all on the same basic 'structure' (unlike dogs, which have a MUCH more plastic genome), and vary little in basic structure and behavior, even in species as divergent as Amur Tigers (aka "Siberian" tigers) or the Sand Cat. A cat is a cat is a cat, and you can see the same behaviors in big cats as you see in domestic cats. And 'brown ticked' or 'brown mackerel' patterns are kind of the 'cat default' pattern. Almost everything else is a mutation. It's mostly true of rabbits, mice, rats, etc. as well. Ticked pattern is often called "wild type", and everything else is a variation on that.

Melodi Grundy: From a farmer's or smallholders PRACTICAL viewpoint, what they need to know is that these very large cats exist, will interbreed with their domestic females and the kittens MUST be tamed early and often. Even then some may simply prove too wild to be around wild stock and do best as the semi-domesticated pet for a very special owner (like my old professor who was happy to live a bachelor life with 35 pounds plus of muscle and feline independence). They are sadly often put down by farmers because while they can make the very best mousers, some also become livestock killers. The same was true originally of Maine Coons and Norwegian Forest Cats; in fact, both breeds were often considered "vermin" by the farmers of Maine and Scandinavia. And an adult Forest Cat who has not been duly and early traumatized by chickens will take poultry.

Jay Bangle: Cats are not truly domestic animals, in the conventional sense. WE didn't take a cat and breed it to our needs - as we did with every other domestic species. Cats found a symbiotic relationship with humans and adopted us. Actual breeding of cats is only a little over 100 years old. By comparison, dogs have been purposely bred for 14,000 years (give or take), goats for about 10,000 years, horses about 5,000 years.

Melodi Grundy: Most farmers and smallholders end up with half-domestics/half wildcat crosses, and usually the domestic cat half allows for domestication with a bit of work but not always.

Jay Bangle: Again, the line is very ambiguous as to what constitutes a "domestic" cat. I would prefer you not confuse true "wildcats" with what we consider "domestic" cats. In almost every case you are talking about, it is *Felis catus*" or domestic cats, not any of the F. silvestris. It's really hard to explain to lay people. More confusion doesn't help. "Feral" is the preferred term for F. catus that doesn't depend on humans. Linnean names are the best. (Bobcats are "Lynx rufus", FYI).

Melodi Grundy: Jay knows more than I do about the current state of this - the "Pixie Bob" Breed is believed to actually be a cross between this "mystery X" Cat and generic domestic cats; although the popular belief is that they are crossed with bobcats.

Jay Bangle: We don't have any native F. silvestris in the New World. Every cat in the US that isn't true New World cat species, or a deliberate cross with an Old World wild cat species, is F. catus - purely. NWC and OWC don't hybridize - at least not more than a single generation (the same is true for horses & donkeys. The only fertile mules produce pure horses or pure donkeys, by accident of genetic mixing. And again ONLY FEMALES are ever even remotely fertile. No male mules have ever reproduced. Doesn't help that the vast majority of them are gelded - but the science is consistent that even if none of them were, none of them would reproduce).

Melodi Grundy: Actually it is exactly the sort of information I am interested in as I'm trying to re-write this chapter so honestly how would you suggest I frame this is an easy to read and understand manner for someone like a lady on my forum (that helped inspire the book) when her barn cat Momma was "screaming from the barn" and produced two giant brown-ticked tabby kittens with no tails and giant back legs. The vet came over and said, "Killed the mother in kitten birth, right?" My friend said "No, she lived but there was a lot of screaming from the barn."

Jay Bangle: Big kitten, first time mom - you do the math. It's really not as uncommon as people think to have a single, giant kitten. Litter sizes of 4 are really the best. No one kitten gets too big to be born.

Melodi Grundy: I helped talk her through how to tame them as they grew. One was very, wild and eventually ran off; the other one became a huge (30 pounds) of muscle and brains. Independent, but an extremely good mouser for years.

Jay Bangle: Just an independent-minded, unsocial (genetically, probably) domestic cat.

Melodi Grundy: My comparison and speculation on the Maine Coons/Forest Cats is that both are domestic cats that "went wild" for 200 to 500 years on different sides of the Atlantic. Both got to be rather huge and furry (living in harsh climates): one became a loner and the other lives in prides in the wilds of Norway.

Jay Bangle: They are pure domestic cats - both. It's what's called a "Natural Breed", they come from a particular area, and are the "random-bred cats", or "naturally occurring" feral cats of a particular area. Other breeds are British Short hair, Japanese Bobtail, Turkish Van, American Short hair, Chartreux (French Blue), etc. TICA (The International Cat Association) will accept into the Stud Book, any cat that substantially looks like the standard requires and has the right paperwork from the specific area in question. So, if you're running around Norway and find a good-looking feral cat that fits the Norwegian Forest Cat standard well enough (3 AB judges have to sign a form) - boom, there it is. It's not very common for many breeds, but the Thai (an old-school Siamese look - not quite Apple Head, but certainly not the guided missile look of the modern Siamese) is the one where it's still being done. But none of them are true "wild cats". All are F. catus.

A study conducted by Dr. Leslie A. Lyons of the Gilbreath-McLorn Endowed Professor of Comparative Medicine showed that: "The Pixie-Bobs are not hybrids. Very cool looking cats, but not bobcat derivatives." (Dr. Lyons) For information on the genome testing and the data collected by the Feline Genetics and Comparative Medince Labratory visit:
http://felinegenetics.missouri.edu

Melodi Grundy: But their genetics are domestic cats; I didn't have a clue what the status of the "Mystery Cats" was these days or what to call them; I only know they exist and they are a special situation that many smallholders are likely to encounter, especially cross-breeds if they insist on having (or adopting) a pregnant female.

Jay Bangle: "Legend Cats" is what they are generally called by the PB [Pixie Bob] people.

Pixie Bob information: http://www.agentcats.com, http://www.catconcerns.com/pixie-bob/

Polydactyl Cats (Hemingway Cats): https://www.cat-world.com.au/polydactyl-cats.html

APPENDIX II
FOR I WILL CONSIDER MY CAT JEOFFRY"

Christopher Smart, from Jubilate Agno (written between 1759-63; Smart was confined in a mental institution at that time, with no companionship or friendship save for that of his cat Jeoffry).

For I will consider my Cat Jeoffry.
For he is the servant of the Living God duly and daily serving him.
For at the first glance of the glory of God in the East he worships in his way.
For this is done by wreathing his body seven times round with elegant quickness.
For then he leaps up to catch the musk, which is the blessing of God upon his prayer.

For he rolls upon prank to work it in.
For having done duty and received blessing he begins to consider himself.
For this he performs in ten degrees.
For first he looks upon his forepaws to see if they are clean.
For secondly he kicks up behind to clear away there.
For thirdly he works it upon stretch with the forepaws extended.
For fourthly he sharpens his paws by wood.
For fifthly he washes himself.
For sixthly he rolls upon wash.
For seventhly he fleas himself, that he may not be interrupted upon the beat.

For eighthly he rubs himself against a post.
For ninthly he looks up for his instructions.
For tenthly he goes in quest of food.
For having consider'd God and himself he will consider his neighbour.
For if he meets another cat he will kiss her in kindness.
For when he takes his prey he plays with it to give it a chance.
For one mouse in seven escapes by his dallying.

For when his day's work is done his business more properly begins.

For he keeps the Lord's watch in the night against the adversary.

For he counteracts the powers of darkness by his electrical skin and glaring eyes.

For he counteracts the Devil, who is death, by brisking about the life.

For in his morning orisons he loves the sun and the sun loves him.

For he is of the tribe of Tiger.

For the Cherub Cat is a term of the Angel Tiger.

For he has the subtlety and hissing of a serpent, which in goodness he suppresses.

For he will not do destruction, if he is well-fed, neither will he spit without provocation.

For he purrs in thankfulness, when God tells him he's a good Cat.

For he is an instrument for the children to learn benevolence upon.

For every house is incomplete without him and a blessing is lacking in the spirit.

For the Lord commanded Moses concerning the cats at the departure of the Children of Israel from Egypt.

For every family had one cat at least in the bag.

For the English Cats are the best in Europe.

For he is the cleanest in the use of his forepaws of any quadruped.

For the dexterity of his defence is an instance of the love of God to him exceedingly.

For he is the quickest to his mark of any creature.

For he is tenacious of his point.

For he is a mixture of gravity and waggery.

For he knows that God is his Saviour.

For there is nothing sweeter than his peace when at rest.

For there is nothing brisker than his life when in motion.

For he is of the Lord's poor and so indeed is he called by benevolence perpetually—Poor Jeoffry! poor Jeoffry! the rat has bit thy throat.
For I bless the name of the Lord Jesus that Jeoffry is better.

For the divine spirit comes about his body to sustain it in complete cat.
For his tongue is exceeding pure so that it has in purity what it wants in music.
For he is docile and can learn certain things.
For he can set up with gravity which is patience upon approbation.

For he can fetch and carry, which is patience in employment.
For he can jump over a stick which is patience upon proof positive.
For he can spraggle upon waggle at the word of command.
For he can jump from an eminence into his master's bosom.
For he can catch the cork and toss it again.
For he is hated by the hypocrite and miser.

For the former is afraid of detection.
For the latter refuses the charge.
For he camels his back to bear the first notion of business.
For he is good to think on, if a man would express himself neatly.
For he made a great figure in Egypt for his signal services.

For he killed the Ichneumon-rat very pernicious by land.
For his ears are so acute that they sting again.
For from this proceeds the passing quickness of his attention.
For by stroking of him I have found out electricity.
For I perceived God's light about him both wax and fire.
For the Electrical fire is the spiritual substance, which God sends from heaven to sustain the bodies both of man and beast.
For God has blessed him in the variety of his movements.
For, tho he cannot fly, he is an excellent clamberer.
For his motions upon the face of the earth are more than any other quadruped.
For he can tread to all the measures upon the music.
For he can swim for life.
For he can creep.

Resources

Suggested Books

Cat Facts: The Pet Parents A-to-Z Home Care Encyclopaedia: Kitten to Adult, Disease & Prevention, Cat Behavior Veterinary Care, First Aid.

Galaxy, Jackson. Total Cat Mojo: *The Ultimate Guide to Life with Your Cat* (Tarcherperigee: 2017). Understanding your cats' behaviors and how most effectively to interact with them.

Little, Susan E., ed. *The Cat: Clinical Medicine and Management* (St. Louis: Elsevier, 2012). Probably the most comprehensive single veterinary overview of cat care.

Newman, Aline Alexander, and Gary Weitzman. *How to Speak Cat: A Guide to Decoding Cat Language (National Geographic Children's Books: 2015).* A particularly good starter for children (or adults) who are not already closely familiar with cats, and a delight for children (or adults) who are cat-lovers.

Richter G. *Ultimate Pet Health Guide* (Hay House, 2017). A guide written by a veterinarian which also covers a number of issues such as herbal remedies (and much of what we know about cannabis dosage, constituents, and efficacy for various conditions in cats and dogs).

Thomas, Elizabeth Marshall. *The Tribe of the Tiger: Cats and Their Culture* (New York: Simon & Schuster, 1994). One of the best guides to why your cats act the way they do.

"Brever, Melissa. 'Cats at Sea: 7 Famous Seafaring Felines'. MNN.com (website), April 26, 2012. https://www.mnn.com/family/pets/stories/cats-at-sea-7-famous-seafaring-felines

Poison Control: if your pet has eaten something they should not have or if you're worried that your pet has been poisoned, these numbers are available. There is a small fee for calling, but the Pet Poison Helpline has a very large searchable database on the various poisons and their visible effects.

United States, Canada, Caribbean: (855) 764-7661.
https://www.petpoisonhelpline.com/poisons/

United Kingdom: 0044-1202 50 90 00.
https://vpisglobal.com

The World Veterinary Association: has a list of all members. If you need to locate a veterinarian elsewhere in the world, this is a good resource.

Belgium: 0032 2 533 70 20.
http://www.worldvet.org/index.php

The Kitten Lady: extremely useful website on feeding and caring for kittens. She includes videos and has published two books on the subject of fostering kittens; http://www.kittenlady.org/about/

The International Cat Association (TICA): https://www.tica.org

The Cat House on the Kings: https://www.cathouseonthekings.com

Vet Street: http://www.vetstreet.com

Jackson Galaxy: https://www.jacksongalaxy.com/

International Animal Rescue: https://www.internationalanimalrescue.org/

Animal League: https://www.animalleague.org/what-we-do/rescue/international-pet-rescue/

The Anti-Cruelty Society: https://anticruelty.org

Cats International: https://catsinternational.org

International Cat Care: https://icatcare.org/nurses/felinefocus

The Purr Company: http://www.thepurrcompany.com/cat-articles.php

Cat Health: https://www.cathealth.com

Orphan Kitten Club: http://orphankittenclub.org

Best Friends: https://bestfriends.org/resources/cats

BIBLIOGRAPHY

Banks, T.J. "Feline Heroes: the Cats of World War I". Petful (website); May 22 (2017). https://www.petful.com/behaviors/cats-world-war/

Brøndegaard, V.J. Folk og fæ 2: Dansk husdyr etnologi (Copenhagen: Rosenkilde og Bagger, 1992).

Emmons, George Thornton; with Jean Lowe. The Tlingit Indians (Washington: Washington University Press, 1991).

Grimm, Jakob. Teutonic Mythology, 4 vols. Tr. by James Stallybrass (London: Dover, 1966).

Hamper, Beth, Joe Bartges, Claudia Kirk, Angela L. Witzel, Maryanne Murphy , and Donna Raditic. "The Unique Nutritional Requirements of the Cat: A Strict Carnivore". In The Cat: Clinical Medicine and Management, ed. Susan E. Little (St. Louis: Elsevier, 2012), pp. 236-41.
Harasen, Greg L.G., and Susan E. Little. "Musculoskeletal Diseases", in The Cat: Clinical Medicine and Management, ed. Susan E. Little (St. Louis: Elsevier, 2012), pp. 704-33.

Holtsmark, Anne, "Kattar Sonr", Sagabook XVI 2-3 (1963-4), pp. 144-55.

Kaffashi ER, Khayat NH, Mahmoudi J. "Comparative Study of Valeriana Offinalis Root Extract, Diazepam, and Ketamine on CNS Depressive Effects in Cats". Veterinary Clinical Pathology (Veterinary Journal Tabriz); Winter 2012, 5:4(20); pp. 1407-17.

Lewis, C.W. The Problem of Pain (Centenary Press: 1940).

The Life and Adventures of a Cat. Anon., variously attributed to Henry Fielding and/or William Guthrie (Willoughby Mynors: 1760. Rep. Gale ECCO, Print Editions: 2010).

Little, Susan E., ed. The Cat: Clinical Medicine and Management (St. Louis: Elsevier, 2012).

Luther, M. The Life and Letters of Martin Luther. Ed. Preserved Smith (London: Murray, 1911).

Lyons, Leslie A. "Email from Dr. Lyons, regarding the Pixie Bob" 2018

Ludwig, Robi. "Helping Kids Deal with the Loss of a pet" (June 2017) https://www.care.com/c/stories/3450/helping-kids-deal-with-the-loss-of-a-pet/
Murray, Kevin. "Catslechta and Other Mediaeval Material Relating to Cats". Celtica 125 (2007), pp. 123-160.

Nanna Gunnarsdóttir. "Cats of Reykjavík and Iceland's Christmas Cat". Guide to Iceland (website): 2018. https://guidetoiceland.is/connect-with-locals/nanna/iceland-s-christmas-cat-and-cats-of-reykjavik

Rachewiltz, Boris de. An Introduction to Egyptian Art: 3000 Years of Creative Genius, tr. R.H. Boothroyd (London: Spring 1966).

Richter G. Ultimate Pet Health Guide (Hay House, 2017).

Rincon, Paul. "Dig discovery is oldest 'pet cat'" [BBC on-line edition, Thursday, 8 April,2004, 18:00 GMT 19:00 UK].

Snorri Sturluson. Edda Snorra Sturlusonar [n.ed.], 3 vols. (Osnabrück: Otto Zeller 1848-87).

Thomas, Elizabeth Marshall. The Tribe of The Tiger: Cats and Their Culture (New York: Simon & Schuster, 1994) [with special acknowledgment for her excellent insights on how cats view territories within a barnyard].

Tyldesley, Joyce. Daughters of Isis: Women of Ancient Egypt (London: Penguin, 1994).

Vatnsdoela saga, ed. Einar Ól. Sveinsson. Íslenzk fornrit VIII (Reykjavík: Hið íslenzka fornritafélag, 1939).

van Vechten, Carl. The Tiger in the House (1936; rep. Courier Corp., 1996).

Vermeulen, Nico. The Complete Encyclopedia of Herbs (Toronto: MGR Publishing, 1998).

Wynne, Susan G., and Barbara Fougere. Veterinary Herbal Medicine (Elsevier Health Sciences, 2006).

Melodi Lammond-Grundy grew up in California and went to college at the University of Southern Mississippi. She spent some years in Colorado, then moved to San Francisco, where she was, for a time, a member of the well-known household and writers' community. She has been in the pagan/heathen community since the 1990's and has degrees in both history and anthropology. In her spiritual life she has studied she has studied spae-craft, a form of trance-based native Germanic divination. A spákona is the diviner, not the art of divination. Which she learned from Diana Paxson. She still practices divination and psychic readings to this day, lending herself to speak about current events. Her writing skills were first shown in several on line publications, followed by co-authoring the Falcon Dream Trilogy. Melodi was one of the first authors to come on-board at Three Little Sisters, and we are pleased to be able to present both her non-fiction work and her upcoming Atlantis novel.

The Three Little Sisters

The Three Little Sisters is an indie publisher that puts authors first. We specalize in the strange and unusual. From titles about pagan and heathen spirituality to traditional fiction we bring books to life.

https://the3littlesisters.com

www.ingramcontent.com/pod-product-compliance
Lightning Source LLC
Chambersburg PA
CBHW051518120626
46551CB00012B/980